Dedication

This book is dedicated to my future unborn daughter Wisdom Sophia Monet; Mommy loves you. Know that way before your father and I chose to conceive you, I prayed and spoke over you. I worked hard, and made plans with God, to ensure that you would have a great legacy. I pray that you will be the best version of who God has created and mandated you to be. That you will love and serve God with your whole heart. That you will be loving, respectful, intelligent, passionate, kind, forward thinking and funny. But most of all, you will embrace your authentic self. Never forget Wisdom, "...For unto whomsoever much is given, of [her] shall be much required..."
(Luke 12:48).

Acknowledgements

I would like to thank God for giving me the honor and divine ability to write this book. Without God, this would have been an impossible task.

To my momma, Ms. Wright, who taught me how to encourage myself, to be the best, how to be a leader, a speaker, a poet, and a fighter, but most of all how to be "greatness in motion," for which I am thankful.

My grandmothers, Fannie Gentles and Betty Wright: thank you for all of your love, life lessons, prayers, and prophecies you spoke over my life. Thank you for always being there to encourage me and propel me into greatness.

To my SMOTHER, my sister/mother Granada L. Allen, who has always invested, encouraged, empowered, and believed in me, thank you for all the sacrifices you have made on our behalf as your siblings. I truly appreciate your selflessness to ensure I could give birth to my purpose, without altering my destiny. You are my [S]hero.

To my brothers, Jeremy Henry and Henry Allen, you may be gone; however, you will never be forgotten. I will always carry both of you in my heart and in my spirit.

To my sisters Tonya Allen, Carolyn Allen, and Michelle Allen, thanks for your love and support. To my amazing brothers Frederick Allen and Terry Allen, thank you for being excellent examples of Godly men, fathers, and husbands. Thank you for your love, support, wisdom, and always making me laugh.

To my mentors, friends, and family (especially my aunts and uncles), thank you for always taking the time to teach me how to become a better person, minister, author, and woman.

To my nieces and nephews know that the second best title I have ever had is, "Auntie Nell!" I am so proud of each of you! Remember I am always a phone call, a text, an email, and a prayer away from all of you.
♥ Auntie Nell.

Thank you to my editors for all of your support, and your extra sets of eyes.

Lastly, I want to thank the student workers and staff at Cannon Memorial, on the beautiful campus of Saint Leo University. It would be an injustice not to pay homage to you. Thank you for all of your support and allowing the library to be my safe haven and writing oasis.

Foreword

It is my privilege to recommend this book to you. I believe it is really a literary work written with the guidance and aid of the Holy Spirit. The words jotted on these pages are truly revealing and speak of the struggle and honesty of its author.

Tanell Vashawn Allen is a gifted Woman of God, who has spent more than ten years traveling throughout the United States hosting empowerment conferences. Her life has been one message that demonstrates the power of God to create something beautiful out of ashes. I consider myself a friend and a mentor who has had the pleasure of watching Tanell as she continues to spread out her wings to fly higher into her destiny.

In this book, Tanell is very transparent as she boldly shares her life story, not just as a woman, but as a minister of the gospel. She dares to tackle those subjects that are thought of as taboo in society and in the church. She exposes some of the common mistakes that most Christian women make when selecting and dating their mates. This book confronts some of the hidden strongholds that plague single ministers. Hidden sins are real, and they are dealt with in these pages.

I truly believe that the words written in this book are timely and needed. It is a powerful contribution to the body of Christ.

-Apostle Tammy T. Willis,

"LET THE CHURCH SAY AMEN"
CONFESSIONS OF A SINGLE MINISTER
Mocha in My Coffee Publishing Company

By: Tanell Vashawn Allen M.Div.

Table of Contents

Confessions of a Single Minister

Introduction

Let the Church Say Amen: "Confessions of a Single Minister." Confess or confession! Hmm... Why should I? I asked. What has been my success and order of procession in life? The poet in me wants to be deep. The minister within me needs to be theologically and politically correct; one wrong image of me, or confession could be the end of my ministry, but the real me, the Christian woman inside of me, wants to be honest and transparent before God and you. Walking in my deliverance from sexual strongholds and yielding to God has been a serious battle for me.

I remember trying for years in my own might to get past these strongholds and never being able to do so. I constantly felt as if I was in a state of condemnation. The devil constantly reminded me that I was a failure and a hypocrite. It took the power of God, through the Holy Spirit, to break these strongholds and to help me get past those feelings that were contrary to who and what I really was. If I can do it through the Holy Spirit, so can you. It is only through the Holy Spirit, fasting and praying, renewing your mind with the word of God, and being honest with yourself that this transformation can take place. After all, the truth will make us free. Isn't that what confession is all about? James 5:6, encourages us to confess our faults to one another.

Catholic Christians confess their sins to a priest while sitting inside of a box. Jesus becomes the high priest of all who have given their lives to God. I do not want you to be my priest; yet, if you will allow me to use you and my growing pains in this book as my box for confession, we can explore my journey of self-discovery and call to ministry.

My first acknowledgment is that even as a minister, I have missed the mark of God. Daily, I sin. Daily, I struggle with my flesh. In the words of my friend Dee, I have a sexual appetite. To be honest, I never thought about it as an appetite; however, all I know is that I felt free once I confessed this to my friend. I felt free because finally I was able to express what I was going through without feeling ashamed, judged, or condemned.

Now I had someone who would hold me accountable to walk out my deliverance in love, through prayer, and the word of God. The trick of the enemy is to keep us from exposing the things we struggle with. As believers, if we are fearful of confessing our sins because of judgment, or embarrassment, the enemy will keep us bound.

The Bible states, "Where two or three are gathered in my name, I am also in the midst" (Matthew 20:18). When believers stop being ashamed of the things they struggle with, seek help and pray, it is a mighty blow to the enemy's camp. There is always power when the saints get together to pray with clean hands and pure hearts, there is freedom and liberation. Oh, did I mention deliverance?

Masturbation is one of those secret sins that holds you in bondage because no one really knows what you are doing except God, you, and Satan. It is just as bad as having a drug addiction or any other addiction, if not dealt with correctly. It pulls you into a fantasy world that alters your perception of reality. It is a secret sin involving your physical body and your imagination. Some people think that it is okay because you are not committing fornication or adultery. The truth is what you are doing is manipulating your own body for self-gratification and grieving the Holy Spirit that lives inside of you.

This fantasy world is so addictive it actually can change who you are, resulting in negative behaviors such as lying, cheating, or stealing. It can cost you everything to chase and fulfill that sexual high. I thought it was okay because only God and I knew about it; but it was not. Sometimes I would be missing in action feeding into this fantasy world. I did not sleep right because I often spent my time lusting after the flesh. Sometimes the slightest thing would trigger this desire. It was almost as if I was a sex addict. For me, masturbation was the safest route to go. I could not get pregnant, no STDs, and no scandal for the good minister.

Although I knew I needed deliverance from this stronghold, it was extremely difficult for me to walk in this deliverance because I had no one to talk to about it. I felt like Apostle Paul when he talked about "the thorn in [his] side" (2 Corinthians 12:7). I could so relate to him when he asserts, "I wanted to do good, but evil is always there." This is the story of most of our lives. For me, "the evil" was a hyper erotic side bursting to be free. I had to learn not to suppress it, but to allow God to deliver me from the lustful parts of it and to show me how to embrace my sexuality without demonizing it. Sex and our sexuality are part of who we are and our lives. How we choose to use it and embrace, it is something completely different.

In order for me to truly experience deliverance and embrace healing, I had to deal with the root of the issues I was struggling with. I trust that my transparency as a child of God, a minister, and a woman will give someone the strength and courage to be set free from lust. Remember, "[We] can do all things through Christ who strengthens [us]" (Philippians 4:13). You will, and you shall get past every addiction that distracts you, robs you of your purpose and destiny, and takes you out of the presence of God.

My prayer for you is that God will cover your mind, heart, and spirit from any spiritual, mental, or emotional setbacks. I also pray that you will be able to use this book as a tool to usher in healing, breakthrough, hope, and encouragement to overcome anything that is stopping you from embracing your deliverance, or your calling in life.

Confessions of My Childhood

Chapter 1

Blemished Fruit

"We are nothing without them, our scars and blemishes..."-Anonymous

For years, I never realized that I was blemished fruit. I knew I had issues, but I did not fully understand what was going on inside of me. Two major issues I had were the fear of rejection and being hurt. As a result, I did not trust people very easily, especially men. I never allowed men to get too close to me. I was never very comfortable with a man having too much access to me or having any control over me.

When I was about four, my half-brother, from time to time, would pluck my pre-ripened fruit from my small and delicate branches. As he climbed my premature tree, he broke, bent, twisted, and pulled on my branches. I remember one particular time he woke me up in the wee hours of the morning and carried me to our father's big blue van. My nightgown was white with little pink flowers and lace across the top. He carried my body in his arms like a limp noodle instead of like a princess being rescued by her knight in shiny armor. I can still feel the cool morning air blowing across my bare feet as they dangled over his arm.

I loved milk as a kid. He tried to wake me by calling my name, but I was a hard sleeper. He then slowly poured milk in my mouth, letting it run down my throat. I remember the cool milk running down my chin and soaking the front of my nightgown. My mind and body were being manipulated before my body ever thought about having a period to regulate it.

 It was not until; I took a poetry class in college that I dealt with the reality of being molested. As a Christian, there was a need to forgive him, move on. I had to learn how to cope with this trauma and not be angry, in order for my blemishes to heal. I had to find the supernatural courage to pardon him to embrace my breakthrough. The poet in me took to writing as a form of therapy. Although, I have forgiven him, I still have scars. I stopped drinking plain milk for a long time. I subconsciously lied to myself for years saying I just preferred chocolate milk. I became a very light sleeper. To this day, if you call my name I usually wake right up. Being molested opened me up to having sexual desires and fantasies prematurely.

My half-brother was sick, and in his sickness, he also molested some of my other siblings and later raped an elderly woman. Knowing that most victims become victimizers or promiscuous helped me deal with the darkness in him. As I forgave him, I wondered to myself, who was his victimizer? What was the story that he would tell?

I never blamed my parents for what happened. Looking back, I think things would have been different if my father had been present rather than absent. His absence created a deficiency in my life physically and emotionally. I always longed to have a relationship with him that left a void only God could fill.

I was blemished in almost every area of my life -- physically, sexually, mentally and emotionally. The molestation was only half of the reason why I was considered blemished fruit. I feel the other half of the reason was because my father was never there to protect me, provide for me, or teach me the things that I was supposed to learn from him.

The truth of the matter is I am not the only person who has discovered that they have blemishes. Most of us have experienced some type of trauma, or have had an experience that has left us with a blemish or two, if we are honest with ourselves. Some people may have suppressed the trauma that they experienced as a coping mechanism.

Pearls of Wisdom

1. The first step to overcoming blemishes is to acknowledge the fact that you have them.

2. The second step is to ask God to show you how to begin to deal with them.

3. The third step is to find an accountability circle to help you heal properly from your blemishes.

4. The fourth step is to be patient with yourself while you are on this journey of healing and transformation.

5. The fifth step is to no longer allow the circumstances and situations that led to your blemishes continue to lord over your life through unforgiveness.

Chapter 2

Things My Daddy Did and Did Not Do

"Being a father is the most important role I will ever play and if I don't do this well, no other thing I do really matters." – **Michael Josephson**

My father worked for the railroad and he was always chasing skirts. The brief moments he was home, he spent terrorizing my mother and reigning fear over us. He was one of the cruelest men I ever met. I remember he kicked my mother in the head with a steel-toed-boot and left her on the floor to bleed to death. My father was malicious. He broke my mother's ring finger on her left hand by twisting it and she never got it straightened out. I do not think my mother ever went to the hospital because to this day her finger still resembles a chicken wing.

As a little girl, I loved playing with my mother's pecan-colored hands. I asked her what happened to her finger, even though I knew my father did it. I said, "Momma why didn't you get your finger fixed?" My momma always took her time when answering me because, as a child, I was super quick at asking endless questions. She knew I was curious about so many things that she had to answer me in a way that satisfied the why factor in my little mind.

My mother gazed out for a moment and sucked in a deep breath before answering me. "Because," she said, "they would have to re-break my finger and that would hurt too much." When my mother said that, I visualized my mother's heart stopping as they snapped her finger back into place because the pain was too intense. That image haunted me as a child.

My mother finally saved up enough money to buy her own car and my father hated that. He would run my mother off the road. Sometimes he would come home and pick a fight with her to have an excuse to leave for days at a time. The best thing my mother ever did was to divorce him.

The only time, I ever remember my father purchasing me anything was during my parent's divorce. He bought me a white Barbie Doll with blonde hair and blue eyes. I was excited to get this epitome of beauty. He bought my sister a boom box and I remember the cassette tape he bought her with this very popular song on it titled, "Freaks Come Out at Night," and he bought my brother a skateboard that he absolutely loved.

My father was intentional about coming to see us that day; maybe it was to impress someone, or to make himself feel good. His purpose for coming to see us and spending time with us was short-lived. I believe my father's motives for coming to see us and buying us those gifts were more to rub his money in my mother's face because he never bought us anything else, or came for scheduled visits again. Whenever we saw him, it was random.

My dad was a man of great means. He worked on the railroad tracks for a long time, so he did have the means to provide and take care of his children, but he rarely did it by choice. One of my older brothers, who had a different mother, asked my father for $16 a week to help take care of him and he said, "No." My father refused to help in any way. His mother took him to child support court and she ended up getting hundreds of dollars a month in child support.

My father was "The Ladies Man." Women flocked after him. He was never faithful to my mother, or any of the other women he married or dated. He was mean, vindictive, and controlling. I knew that any man I married had to be the opposite of my father.

I love my dad, but some of the hardest things I had to do was to accept the fact, that we may never have the father and daughter relationship that I longed to have with him, or share a special bound. I had to accept and forgive him, for not being who, or what I needed him to be as my father. In doing so, I am still learning how to love my father unconditionally and respect him as my dad. It is true he has made many mistakes, but he did do somethings right and that was to co-create my siblings and me.

I had to learn how celebrate him regardless of my personal feelings not just for myself, but for my siblings, for my future husband, and for most of all my children. Maybe he will have a better relationship with his grandchildren than he had with me. My heart has changed because at least now, I am willing to give him another opportunity to try to be a part of my life.

Pearls of Wisdom

1. Love yourself enough not to settle for being just "A Baby Daddy" or "A Baby Momma." Be careful and selective with whom you choose to have children.
2. Being a present, but absent parent, does not help foster positive and healthy relationships with your kids. Make sure you are an active parent inside and outside of your home, and that you take time to engage with your children outside of disciplining and providing for them.
3. Parenting is a full-time job with no sick days and no time off. Make sure you and your partner are fully committed to learning and embracing parenthood.
4. It is hard to love a vindictive person because you never know when they will unleash their rage.
5. When you leave an abusive relationship, never ever go back to it.
6. According to FCADV, "Abuse is about control… Anytime a change occurs, abuse tends to escalate."
7. The National Domestic Violence hot line number (877) 440-0299.

Chapter 3

The Monster in My House

"Whoever fights monsters should see to it that in the process he does not become a monster."
- Friedrich Nietzsche

After my mother divorced my father, it was as if I was seeing her for the first time in my life. She had a beautiful bubbly personality. My mother was the type of person who was the life of the party, made everyone feel welcomed, and helped take care of her siblings. For the first time in my life, I realized she was funny.

I remember feeling happy and free as we left the courthouse in Dade City the day of my parents' divorce was finalized. My mother began to go out to a little bar across the street from our new house called "Mary's Place."

I will never forget when my mother started seeing a man by the name of Jackson. He was tall, thin, good- looking, and charming. He had a warm smile and medium dark brown eyes. His skin was the shade of a rich chocolate brown. Jackson had a full beard that was always well-groomed. The hair on his head only grew in like a convertible, but it did not look bad on him. I think because of his looks and his charming personality, he was able to manipulate and prey on many people.

At first glance, Jackson seemed like Prince Charming. He did not hit my mother; that was the number one thing. Jackson was affectionate, loving, and caring. He helped around the house by cooking, cleaning, he was nice, and well-mannered to everyone who knew him. Yet, something about Jackson was just not right.

He was a type of monster that you hid your little kids from, especially your little girls. He may have fooled many people, but one person he could not fool was my Great Granny-Granny. Now you had to know Great Granny-Granny to know how nobody, I mean absolutely nobody, got anything past her. I mean those switches are a whole other story within itself. You see Great Granny-Granny did not play the radio. Before giving her life to Christ, she was known for three things: switches, whiskey, and her pistol.

I remember one day, she asked me if Jackson had ever touched me. At that moment, I did not remember him touching me, so I said, "No." About 30 minutes later, I heard my Great Granny-Granny confronting Jackson. I secretly, watched from the back of the kitchen as I hid on the side of the wall by the big white stove. She asked, "Nigga you ain't round here messing with these girls, are you?" Before he could answer, Great Granny-Granny replied, "I believe you is, but if I ever find out for sure I'm going to get my pistol and blow your brains out." I looked at Great Granny-Granny as she sat on the couch with a suspicious look on her face.

Her head was cocked slightly to the right side as she squinted her eyes closely together, staring at him, as if she was searching the depths of his soul with her arms folded across her chest. I knew she was not playing. She was his judge and jury and with one wrong move, word, or expression she was going to convict him and kill him. My saying "no" saved his life that day.

I think because I said "no," Jackson got comfortable. A year later while I was sleeping on our living room floor, he tried to wake me. I told him, "Stop! Leave me alone. I'm tired." He tried to stand me up to see if I was awake. My body slumped over to display how tired I was. I must have had too much fun playing outside that day. He lightly slapped my face to see if I would wake up. When I did not respond, he laid me back down. He took the lid off a can of Royal Crown hair grease. He pulled my underwear down and he stuck his finger in the grease to scoop a glob out.

I was semi-conscious, but when I felt his hand touch me, I cried out, "NOOO! STOP!" He did for a few minutes and I drifted back to sleep. A few minutes later, I felt him grinding on top of me. I cannot say for sure he penetrated me, but I can say he touched me inappropriately. By this time, I was more awake and alert. I tried with all my might to push him off from me. My pleading for him to stop went unanswered until I clearly said, "Jackson I am going to tell on you." He got off me quickly.

In my mind, it was hard for me to believe that all of that had occurred. At first, I thought it was a dream until I smelled the hair grease as I wiped the next morning. I remember telling my mom as she played with me outside the next day. I had to be about six. I remember telling her and going back to play as if nothing major had happened. I remember her taking my sister and me to the doctor, but I do not remember anything else. All I know is Jackson never touched me again.

Jackson used to like me to sit on his lap and brush his beard. One day my mother was cooking dinner and she happened to see me sitting on his lap and brushing his beard.

She told me, "Get down!"

I asked, "Why?"

She looked at me and sharply said, "Get down and I am not going to tell you again." By the tone of her voice, I knew I had better listen.

This was at least more than a year after I told my mom about him touching me. I think due to the trauma of that experience and me being so young I subconsciously buried it. It was not until later in my life, when I chose to forgive my abusers that the experiences came back to my recollection.

One Saturday morning, my mother was gone and I accidentally walked in on Jackson using the bathroom. I tried to apologize, but he yelled at me, "Shut the door!" When he finished in the bathroom, he fussed at me. He said, "You knew I was in the bathroom." I started trying to explain to him, "I did not know you were using the restroom?" He replied, "Yes, you did, and you stood there watching." I shook my head no, trying to get him to understand it was an accident. Before I knew what was going on, Jackson took his hand and backslapped me across my face. Warm bright red blood poured from my nose.

A look of shock and panic came across his face. He hurried me to the bathroom to place a cold rag and pressure to my nose as he tilted my head back and apologized. I was not fully sure why he apologized. Maybe he was sorry or maybe because he did not want me to tell my momma. Either way all that was running through my mind like 90 going north was "OHHH I'M GOING TO TELL MY MOMMA!"

My momma had been with Jackson for years. I only recall him having a job once. He may have had two, but I do not remember it. The best thing that ever came from Jackson was my brother Jeremy. I was so happy when my momma told me she was having us a baby. I say "us," but I really mean "me" a baby. In my mind, my brother was my baby. I absolutely adored the fact that I was going to be a big sister for once. My little brother was the most beautiful baby I had ever seen. His skin was the perfect shade of brown; his eyes were brown pools of warmth, when he chose to open them.

He always smelled good, just like a baby should, until he pooped. My mother always kept him clean with Johnson & Johnson baby bath soap and shampoo. She kept Jeremy moisturized and powdered with those products. As she got him ready, I always admired his dark greenish-brown birthmarks on his back and on his leg. I used to love to hold him and wake him up to stare into his eyes. Maybe, this was why my mother stayed with Jackson so long.

Jackson eventually ended up introducing my momma to drugs. This was in the 80's, and crack was a highly addictive social drug in some parts of the Black community. My momma went from getting high occasionally to becoming a functional addict. When we were younger, she would leave us at home and say, "I am going to go see a man about a cow or a dog." We were always so excited that she was going to come back with a cow, or dog. We were happy she was leaving. No matter how many hours she was gone, we tried to wait for her. She never left us over night or for days at a time.

My mother started stealing only on the weekend to earn extra money. She was very good at it and she never got caught; it was just a side hustle. My momma and Jackson broke up and she eventually lost or quit her job. She started shoplifting full-time to support us and her habit. We began to move a lot; almost every year, or every year and a half we moved. My mother was arrested several times for shoplifting and driving with a suspended license. I remember one day I overheard her saying she was high and gotten multiple tickets in one night and threw her driver's license away.

There were times we lived in condemned houses, and we would come home from school to find all of our belongings on the curb. It seemed like my mother went from one bad relationship to another with each man having some form of substance abuse problem, or emotional issues. I vowed never to date or marry anyone like the men my mother dated. Her heart always allowed her to see the best in people regardless of their issues.

As my momma's habit started spinning out of control. It was hard to live with her like that. When she came down off her high, sometimes she was mean, but when she was clean and sober, she was an excellent momma.

She always told me, "Whatever you be, whether negative, or positive, you be the best at it." She would come to my honor roll teas and award ceremonies. There were a couple she was slightly hung-over at, but she would be there. I remember her staying up late with me to help me finish my projects and homework. When I competed in public speaking, she would stand at the back of the room and give me my cues when to talk louder, or clearer.

I remember hearing one of my friends give a speech called, "To Soar." I fell in love with public speaking at that moment. I remember thinking that was good, but I can say it better. I committed myself to learning every word of that three-and-a-half-page speech and saying it for my momma at the age of sixteen. She was truly impressed. She told me, "Say it again." I did. Then, she had me say it in front of some important people and that is how I got into public speaking. My mother has always instilled in me to be a leader, that I am an influencer, to articulate thoughts, and to never allow anyone to silence my voice. She has always supported my gifting and my calling as a minister because she knew, "I Was Made for This."

Years later, my mother asked me why I never told her about Jackson and my half-brother abusing my siblings and me. I said, "Momma I told you about Jackson." She looked so surprised and shocked. I realized she did not know what I was talking about by the look in her eyes. I reminded her of what happened. She said, "Nell I really did not know. Please forgive me. I would have done something." I was not mad at my mother, my father, Jackson, or my half-brother. I simply had let it all go. I was no longer going to be the victim of sexual assault. When I forgave them, I forgave my mother and father for what they did or did not know, as well as for not being there to protect me. I had made up my mind that I was going from victim to victor.

I was not surprised that my mother truly did not remember me telling her about me being molested. My mother had been through a lot of traumatic experiences and situations in her life. The brain has a way of burying things subconsciously as a coping mechanism. Many children are abused at the hands of adults whom they trust. I hope my story will help them usher in the healing and forgiveness they need to move past this traumatic experience and get the help they need. A good therapist does wonders for the soul.

Pearls of Wisdom

1. Always create a clear line of communication with your children so they will know what is and is not acceptable behavior for others to engage in with them.
2. Always ask God to show you the spirit of a person who will have supervised and unsupervised access to your children before leaving them alone with them.
3. Do background checks on people who are around your children. Some may not have a background, but you still have to watch them and check their references.
4. Trust your children if they say they are being touched or abused. Watch for changes in their behavior because they may not verbally say anything. Some common signs include but are not limited to wetting the bed, layering with clothes, rapid changes in their mood, etc...
5.   Call the authorities to investigate any abuse of any kind whether you fully believe it or not.

Chapter 4

I Come from Good Stock

"She made broken look beautiful and strong look incredible. She walked with the universe on her shoulders, and made it look like a pair wings."
-Anonymous

I have always had a special relationship with my grandmother. She has always been a praying woman. As a little girl, I loved staying with her and sleeping in her bed. There was always one problem with that. My grandma would often say, "Oooh, Nell you's a bad sleeper. I'm going to make you a pallet on the floor."

I loved going to my grandma's house. She was the nicest and prettiest woman I had ever seen. Her light skin had been kissed by the sun so much, until it had caramelized to the perfect shade of tan. Most people thought she was my mother in public until I squealed "Grandma," in the stores. She had the uncanny ability to make men and women of different racial groups pay homage to her without fishing for compliments. She always kind-of-politely laughed it off and said, "Thank you." She was a Plain-Jane-type-of-beautiful. She never needed to wear too much makeup, if any.

I used to watch my grandmother every morning creep out of her bed before the sun came up. She would kneel down on the side of her bed and clasp her hands together, bow her head, and pray. Worship was always an intricate part of her life. As a woman of God, she always inspired me and ignited a passion in me to know God for myself. Her dedication to God inspired many.

My grandmother, Fannie L. Gentles was the first Womanist Theologian I knew, before I ever heard of the term. She is the embodiment of what a true minister looks like. She had the heart of a pastor long before she became one. She was always willing and available to pray, to help, or to encourage anyone.

Every Sunday morning, just as the sun was coming up, you could smell Sunday dinner hanging in the air as my grandmother hummed and made Sunday morning breakfast. She made the best pancakes and buttered toast.

The secret to her pancakes was she would use a little oil in the pan causing them to be a little crisp. They were always golden tan with crispy brown edges. Her toast was simple too! She would just put butter on random places on the bread than broiled it in the bottom of the oven. It seems simple, but that was not always the case. Her food was so good because of the love that she put into even the simplest things she did.

My grandmother has a way of making everybody feel welcomed and loved. She always told me, "You are my special girl." She knew I loved staying with her. She said, "If I only had a bush, you would always be welcomed under that bush with me."

My grandma lived in what I refer to as the sugar shack; an old wooden house that used to be painted white. The peeling paint from the wood showed signs of its share of beating over the years from the sun. It looked like sugar dissolving in water. The fading of the wood looked ashy. Eventually my grandma gave the sugar shack a facelift by getting aluminum siding. Although it was the biggest and coldest house I had ever seen, it was my favorite place to go.

The spookiest room in the house was the bathroom. I hated taking a bath by myself. I liked to crack the door so I could hear my grandma humming. I knew as long as I could hear her humming the boogieman would not get me. The bathroom was drafty, and the floor creaked in some places. As a child, I hated my grandmother's bathtub. It was white and cast-iron with claw feet. Nowadays, people will pay top dollar for an antique tub like that. It is funny, but we often do not appreciate things until they are gone. I was secretly sad when my grandmother replaced the old tub in the bathroom. I have great memories of me racing against time in the claw foot tub especially on some of those colder nights when I had to take a full bath. I could not wait to jump in front of the kerosene heater in our living room.

She was always teaching me something directly, or indirectly. My grandma taught me that God has a sense of humor. He just does not always show us because we would take advantage of it. One day, she told me to look up at the sky. It was just before dusk. The sky looked so beautiful. She said, "Do you see all of those different colors in the sky? That just goes to show that God is a God of color."

My mother has many of the same beautiful personality traits as my grandma. She has always been a resilient woman, a soother, and the epitome of strength. I remember before she divorced my father, she used to walk six miles from San Ann, FL to Dade City, FL, carrying me most of the way. My father had three cars in the yard; however, he did not allow my mother to use any of them. I hated the little walking I did have to do. As a preschooler, my mother knew how to engage me to keep my focus away from the walking.

As a kid, I collected shiny coins, so it was only natural that I loved wearing penny loafers. I always loved for my loafers to be shined with Vaseline grease. My mother kept me mesmerized by keeping fresh shiny pennies in those loafers, which I always took out by the end of the day.

I remember having a full-fledged meltdown because someone took one of the bright shiny pennies out of one of my shoes. This was the worst tantrum ever. I am talking about flinging arms and jumping up and down. My aunt tried to silence me by replacing my shiny penny with a dull, old, and dirty penny. That was when I kicked the tantrum up a notch and really started the water works to going. "Hell has no fury like a preschooler having a full-fledged tantrum." My mother saved the day by sliding a bright, shiny, new penny in the slot. Then she picked me up and rocked me on her lap as she hummed and bounced her knee as she said, "Shush-shush" and told me it was okay. My mother and grandmother have always had a way of soothing me when my world was chaotic or intense.

Pearls of Wisdom

1. Never forget that even at your lowest point God loves you, and has positioned at least one person to show you if nothing else, a glimpse of His love for.
2. Never forget that some of the best lessons in life are free, if you choose to listen and apply the wisdom.
3. There is always someone watching and looking up to you to show them the way.
4. Always remember that just because we do not see or know how God has done, or is doing something, that does not mean it will not, or has not worked out for our well-being.

Chapter 5

My Momma Told My Secret

"I thought about how there are two types of secrets: the kind you want to keep in, and the kind you don't dare to let out." - Ally Carter

As a little girl, I did not talk to very many people outside of my family. I was an introvert. The only people I talked to were my grandmother and my mother. They were my secret keepers. My Uncle Mike had a friend, named Drake, who was simply beautiful, and I know men are not beautiful, but he was to me. Drake's skin was the color of dark berries and his teeth white like pearls. When he smiled at me, I always seemed to melt under the warmth of his radiant personality and his charming good looks. I was drawn to him, I tried to avoid him. I remember telling my mother that I liked him and she told him. I felt betrayed. I thought I was going to fall out from embarrassment and I would die a slow and painful death.

He actually thought it was cute that I liked him. Every chance he got, he always recognized my presence with a corny and stupid smile as he sang my name, *"Heeey Nelll."* It did not matter if it was in public or private. He really did not care where he chose to charm me. I say charm because he was flirting with me knowing that I liked him.

One day, I saw him in Dade Oaks while I was with my friend Nae-nae. I wanted to impress him with my bike riding skills. I am not sure what went wrong, but I fell. I hurt myself. I skinned my arm, my knee, and I hurt my hand. When I looked up, I saw him pointing to his friend and laughing at me. The pain in my body could not compare to the humiliation I felt.

I saw him again a few weeks later alone, and he said, *"Heeey Nelll,"* but I did not want to hear it. I had a "no he ain't talking to me" attitude. I first gave him that great silent treatment and then the rolling of the eyes. "I saw you and your friend laughing at me."

"I wasn't laughing at you."

"Yes, you were, and I don't appreciate it. I really hurt myself."

"Nell, I wasn't laughing at you; I am sorry if you were embarrassed."

"Yes, you were! Don't do that again." I liked him too much to stay mad at him. I forgave him. The bruising of my heart and ego were more than my hand, arm, and knee.

I saw him one night and I was so proud of myself, I remember I had done my own nails, and I wanted to impress him. I said, "Drake look at my nails. I just finished them." He took his time admiring them. He gently caressed my fingers as he looked at each one of them and he asked me, "You want to come over to my house with me behind Dade Oaks?"

I wanted to say yes, but I knew I would get in trouble because I was not allowed to go to people's houses outside of my immediate family without permission.

I said, "Nooo, I have to go home and finish my homework." I did not fall for it, but I wanted to. At the time, my fourteen-year-old mind thought we would probably watch a movie and go to first base. I did not know what he was asking or what he was trying to do. I now know he was trying to get me over to his house to have sex with him.

I walked back to my house in the dark with the cool night air beating on my chocolate skin. As I walked home, I thought about how stupid I was to blow off Drake. The more I thought about it, the more I wanted to hang out with him. I had made it back in the house and my sister was not home yet. I quickly ran back to chase him down, but I was too late, he was gone.

At the time, I did not know God's hand was upon my life. I had been saved for a year, I still struggled with a strong spirit of lust. I did not know what it was and no one around me tapped into the spirit to discern what I needed deliverance from. I was not sure either, but I constantly went to the altar to get saved. I knew fundamentally, something was not quite right with me. I thought once I became a Christian, these urges and desires would go away but they did not.

Looking back over that time in my life, I learned a few things that I want to do differently as a parent. My mother's intentions were to protect me by informing Drake how I felt about him, so he would be careful of how he engaged with me. It was not until I was twenty-three that we slept together. We slept together more out of curiosity than sexual desire. The seeds of lust and desire planted years ago had never been plucked. There was absolutely no emotional, or sexual chemistry there. I simply had a childhood crush on him. The woman I am today would never consider liking Drake, or sleeping with him.

Pearls of Wisdom

1. Parents should always protect their children by guarding their hearts, body, mind, and spirit while teaching them to do the same. One way parents can do this is by giving their children promise rings after taking time to teach them the meaning of them.
2. Create an open dialogue with them to be honest. By also guiding and teaching them with wisdom, love, and the Word of God about their bodies, love, sex, and marriage.
3. You should only discuss with your spouse how your underage child feels about someone romantically; never expose your child to public ridicule.
4. Always follow your first mind about people and listen to Holy Spirit.
5. Be careful about flirting, it can plant seeds of desire that you might regret later. To flirt means, "To charm, to persuade, or seduce."

Confessions of a Grown, Sassy Woman & Her Calling to Ministry

Chapter 6

"I Can Do Bad All by Myself"

"I am too positive, to be doubtful, too optimistic to be fearful and too determined to be defeated."-Anonymous

While walking to the bus stop a few blocks from my apartment, I saw a guy walking with his headphones on. He was handsome. I had never seen a man that pretty. I gave him the nickname, "Pretty Tony." Darnell was Puerto Rican and Black. We met at the bus stop, one thing led to another and we ended up seeing each other. At first, I just saw how attractive he was and how much time we spent together. He went to church with me a few times and I thought it was cute that our names rhymed. He had a decent singing voice and we really enjoyed spending time together. He was a very private person, we always spent a great deal of time laughing with each other and smiling at each other like two kids in puppy love.

As the weather got colder, it seemed as though he did the same. He was never a very talkative person; however, he went from talking to me to barely talking to me at all. I was extremely suspicious of him. He started acting very distant. It began to seem as though my house was his crash spot and I was starting to get sick of it. When he came over, all he was beginning to do was sleep, eat, and occasionally sleep with me. I noticed the shift in behavior and was ready to jump off board.

My body started betraying me; I just was not feeling like myself. I have always been a late-night person and early riser, but I started getting tired sooner, sleeping more, urinating frequently, and my period was sporadic. I was in denial for about a month.

I told Darnell, and it made the situation even worse between us. Neither of us was ready for the responsibility of becoming parents.

I told my Aunt Meka, who was very affirming and loving. I said, "I know everybody is going to be so disappointed in me."

She simply replied, "Nell shit, you grown. We will always be here to support you. You are not in this alone."

I was so confused and did not know what to do. I knew that this was not the right order for this to be happening. "A baby!" I cannot have a baby. The more I spoke with my Auntie, the more she began to calm my fears. I was finally beginning to become excited about having my own child to love and teach; yet I could not help feeling disappointed in myself for bring a child into this world without being married.

BOOM-BOOM-BOOM. Who the hell is that knocking on the door like a lunatic? Maybe it is my cousin, who lives next door. I am not in the mood for Sybil's bipolar-split-personality-mess. This is the same fool who broke out my bedroom window a few months ago, then lied and said that I did it. I was so irritated that somebody had the nerve to wake me up to answer the door on one of the coldest days of the year in the Windy City. I peeked through the blinds and decided to yank the door open. I am a true Floridian. I wear flip flops year round in the Mid-west, but today I was no fool. Me and my flip flops were staying in my cozy and warm apt.

Darnell was standing there with an attitude the size of Montana in his white jean pants with a large golden stain.

"This is all your fault."

I looked shocked and curious simultaneously. I asked him, "What are you talking about?"

He replied, "I know you heard me knocking on the door. If you would have come quicker, I would not have had an accident on myself."

I replied, "So let me get this right, it is my fault that as a grown man you peed on yourself because I did not open the door quickly enough? Yeah okay." I was so sick of Darnell. I wished he would just leave me alone, if he did not want to be in a relationship with me. He slept a lot and gave me the cold shoulder when he was not comatose.

While he showered, I thought about what I could do to calm him down as I crawled back in bed under my warm comforter. It was so cold outside that morning; Chicago's nickname should have been the Frozen City instead of the Windy City. I laughed under my breath as I thought about that wind chill, freezing Darnell's *pissy* pants. "Good!" I thought aloud to myself.

He got in bed quietly, turning his back to me. As cold as it was, there was too much space between us, so I decided to cuddle up close to him. I asked him, "What's wrong? Did something happen at work? Lately, you have not been yourself."

He replied, "It's nothing."

I knew he was lying and shutting me out. I rubbed my hands down his chest playfully, but he groaned and shrugged me off. This hurt more than the lie he had just told me. I felt very much rejected because I was not able to seduce him to get the attention and affection I lived for from him. I equated a man wanting to sleep with me as desiring me, which, in return, made me feel attractive, worthy of love, desirable, and accepted. Having been rejected all my life, I needed the man I slept with to accept me.

I could not take lying in bed next to him one more moment. I got out of bed. Paddling my way across the floor, I put on a pair of my wide leg jeans. I also put my coat on over my silk nightgown. I balled up the brown paper bag that housed two at-home pregnancy tests and stuck them in my coat pocket as I slid my feet into my gym shoes without socks. I went into the bathroom to have a private meeting with my Father. "God, if I am pregnant, take my child to heaven because I don't want to be tied to this fool for the rest of my life." I began to sob uncontrollably over the reality of me having a child with a man I was not married to, not in love with, and not very happy with. I knew I was out of God's will and plan for my life, but I did not know what to do other than pray.

I opened the front door, stepped out to the sidewalk and started walking down the walkway of my nine-unit apartment complex. I quickly crossed Vincennes Street, to head to my closest client's house. We had become close since I started doing her hair. I just had to get out of the house. I was too nervous to take the test at home and did not want to mess up the results.

This was my first time ever taking a pregnancy test. I never dreamed that I would be doing this without my husband standing by the doorway supporting me emotionally and physically. I told myself my bladder must have been nervous too because I had been sitting for a moment not able to pee on the stick. I silently prayed, "God please let it be negative." I finally was able to pee on the stick.

I guess God was like, "Come on, let the suspense be over before this girl becomes undone." I watched the test very closely deciphering and trying to discern the next move of my life. I guess I was watching too hard. There is a cliché that says, 'a watched pot will not boil." I needed to know if the test was positive, or negative. I could not believe my life hung in the balance of this simple arithmetic. If it was a minus sign, no baby; if it was a plus sign, oh baby. I was going to have a baby.

I tried to silence the voice in my head and deny all the symptoms I was having. I told myself a baby was the last thing I needed. I cannot afford to take care of one. I am a struggling hair stylist who works long and crazy hours. I barely make enough money to support myself, let alone a child. I felt a wave of peace come over me, like never before in that moment. I heard in my spirit, "It is ok."

 I looked at the test, finally okay with seeing the plus sign, only to discover that it was negative. I was so relieved, yet at the same time, it was saddening because I wondered what kind of mother I would have been and if I would ever have an opportunity to be a mother. I told myself in God's divine timing, when I am married and more stable, I will have a chance to be a mother. I want to feel like my child is a blessing to me and not a burden. In my mind, my child was a girl, so I referred to her as "she" and "her." I knew I would not have always thought of her as a burden, but at that stage in my life, she would have been.

My aunt said, "When the body thinks it is pregnant, it will sometimes give you symptoms to make you believe you are pregnant." I never said anything different. Some might say it was the stress from my job and the relationship, but I knew differently. I believe I was pregnant and God honored my request. I walked back home knowing that I had to do some damage control. I knew Darnell's season was up in my life and it was time for me to let him go.

As I crept back into bed with my back turned to him, I told him, "I took a pregnancy test." It was as if he stopped breathing. I felt his body freeze and stiffen up. Maybe he did not want to be connected to me for the rest of his life, either. He never asked me what the result was directly. He just replied, "And?" I chewed on the right side of my bottom lip and said, "It was negative." I expected him to roll over and console me, or at least check on me to see how I was processing all this, but he did not. I never felt so alone and lonely in all my life. I vowed to myself I would never allow myself to feel this way again. Wet, warm, silent, tears slid down my face unto my pillow as I cried and prayed myself to sleep that night.

The next morning, I woke up, and it was as if God had taken away all the heaviness. The weather felt so much warmer and lighter outside. I even felt warmer and lighter. I was up getting ready to iron my clothes for my first day of work for my new job. I was so ready to experience something different. I woke Darnell up so he could get the hell out of my house. He was not going to stay in my house and sleep all day while I was at work. He was really one of those "Pretty Tony" types of guys, I always beat him getting ready. I wanted him up, ready, and out of my house. I was not about to let him make me late for my first day of work at the new salon.

I was so excited to start working with my friend Tia on 79th and Saint Lawrence. I knew I would make more money at that salon because of its location, and I was excited that it was also next to the barbershop. I knew it would make it a safer place to work.   The salon where I previously worked had been robbed a few times at gunpoint. It was a blessing that I was never around when that occurred.   It was on a side street off 79th street, which was not good for safety, or business if you relied on walk-ins to build up your clientele because it was not on the main strip. I smiled to myself as I thought about working at my new nail and hair stations.

Finally, I could do hair and nails without feeling as though I had to choose between the two. Darnell angrily snapped, "What?" Pulling me back into reality that I had called him over five minutes ago, I replied in the I am not playing with you voice, "You need to get up and be ready in 15 minutes to leave my house when I leave." I could tell he was mad, but I did not give a fat baby's behind. I knew Darnell was tired and that he had been working a lot, not because he told me that, but because I called his job to investigate.

At first, I did not believe he had a job. I called three White Castles on the Southside of Chicago before I found the one where he worked. I believe in that scripture "a man who does not work does not eat" (2 Thessalonians 3:10).   To add my personal twist to it, his lazy butt will not be dating me either. If a man ever wanted to get rid of me, all he had to do was to ask me for some money.

I looked over my shoulder to call Darnell. I said, "Darnell, look we need to talk." He looked at me as if he was utterly disgusted. I said, "Yesterday, I did not feel like you were acting like a mature man, or even my man when I needed you the most. I took a pregnancy test and you never bothered to ask me what the results were or see how I felt about it. That hurt me."

He replied, "I never said I was your man."

WOW!!! BAE-BAE that statement was gut--wrenching to hear. I felt like he kicked me in the stomach. I began to grab his things, and said, "Since you are not my man, get the hell out of my house and my life." I was too upset to cry.

He noticed I had thrown his beloved Walkman, coat, and personal belongings out the front door, and something in him snapped. Darnell was a very quiet and soft-spoken man. I was so surprised when he flipped the switch in him and he picked up the hot iron and threw it across the living room. It hit the other side of the living room wall and shattered into pieces.

Something must have snapped in me too. I had to release my inner girl version of the Hulk. I picked up the biggest piece of the iron and I began hitting and pushing him out the front door. I knew why I reacted like that. It was out of fear and rage from watching my mother being abused physically at the hands of my father. I promised myself I would never be a domestic violence victim. Yet, it never crossed my mind that if I did not deal with the anger and rage that comes over me at times that I could easily become the victimizer.

In my mind, I always saw the victimizer as male because my father was a man and my mother was his victim. I wish I could say that Darnell was the last man I hit, but he was not. I soon learned a few slaps later that I was turning into my father. One cost me a great guy and from that day forth I have not hit an intimate partner.

Most men who experience domestic violence never talk about it, or they justify it as their partner being crazy. They rarely seek outside help. This is a major issue that must be addressed. It is not acceptable for children of victims or victims to become victimizers.

Back to Darnell, once he was outside and collected his belongings, he soon discovered that he was missing his wallet, and I discovered that he burned the cheap tan carpet in my apartment. This was my first apartment. It was not anything spectacular to anyone, but me. I loved it because it was mine. My cream and tan dining room set came from K-mart, and the rest of my furniture came from a garage sale that my Grandma Foxy saw advertised in a newspaper. My apartment was cream, sage, and tan. I had the ugliest floral print couch and loveseat, with a three-piece taupe antique table set for my living room furniture.

When I walked back to the ironing board and stared at *this* big dumb iron print that was ingrained into my carpet, I thought, "I know he does not think he is getting his damn wallet back. He is not getting his wallet back until he pays for my carpet. I do not know who the hell he thinks he is." My cousin, who lived next door, heard all of the commotion and came over to see what was going on. She walked past him and rolled her eyes silently, daring him to do something. He knew my cousin was bipolar and very violent. He saw and heard her in action several times.

"Uh Tanell, what the hell is going on over *herrre*."

I explained everything to her from his recent mood swings, to him pissing on himself, to his behavior about the pregnancy test, to his latest insult.

My cousin and I were total opposites and were not extremely close, but we always had each other's back with us living next door to each other. "I am about to call Grandma and if he comes over here with that bullshit, I'm going to kick his ass myself." It was visible that the fight shook me up a bit. My cousin told my Grandma Foxy what happened. She then passed me the phone and said, "Grandma *wanna* talk to you Tanell." Now my Grandma in Chicago was different from my Grandma Fannie in FL.

Grandma Foxy was light-skinned, pretty, plus size, shorter, with tiny ears, and a smile that beautifully adorned her face. I loved my grandma's gap in the front of her teeth. She had the prettiest head of salt and pepper hair with a silver halo across the front of her hairline. Her nickname was Foxy from her glory days. When she was younger, she was very glamorous, full-figured, a brick house with a flat stomach and big thighs. Oh, do not get me wrong; she still was glamorous and beautiful when she chose to dress up.

My nickname for her was The Silver Fox. I never met anyone like her. She was indeed, "Ghetto Fabulous." She never pulled any punches and gave great advice most of the time. She could tell you how to do anything and where to go to get the resources you needed.

"Tanell, that nigga *aint* shit. Don't you start at that new salon today? Get your stuff ready and I'm coming to get you."
My grandmother was a doer. My Auntie Meka always told me, "Nell, if I need something done, Momma is the one I go to. She will get it done." She was my step-grandmother, but in our home the only steps that really mattered were the ones that took us up and down the stairs. I was closer to her than I was to my biological grandfather.

My grandfather *Sonny* loved me in his own way; we just were not as close as my grandmother and I were. She always took time to listen to me and made sure I had everything I needed. My Aunt Meka called next, and I began to calm down more as I talked to her. She could tell I was still shaken up. Meka allowed me to stay the night at her house. I ended up staying a week. I had bad dreams the first few days there. I would wake up crying in my sleep. I did not want to go home because Darnell was stalking me. I was scared and fearful of what he might do to my apartment, or me.

After a week, I decided to go home, enough was enough! I could not continue to hide out at my Auntie Meka's house. My cousin would always see him around my apt while I was at work. I always watched my back and went into my house quickly. I would push my dining room table across my back door because my back door was broken, and my landlord and apartment manager were both slum lords, the chances of them repairing the door were slim to none. My grandfather, aka Mr. Gadget, had said he was coming to fix it for almost a year. My grandmother made sure he came this time.

I got tired of looking over my shoulders. I decided to give Darnell back his wallet. There was a gentle knock on the door while I was making myself some dinner one night. When I saw it was him I was not as fearful as I had been.

"Hey Tanell, how are you? I don't mean to bother you. I was trying to see if we can talk and if I could get my wallet back?"

I gave him a long silent pause, while I took my time to think it over. If I open this door, this fool may try to kill me, but if I give him his wallet, maybe he will leave me alone. Damnit, I am going to lose my security deposit. Even if I keep the wallet, there is no guarantee he will pay to replace the damaged carpet.

"Ok, so I will give you your wallet back, but I don't trust you to let you in my home, or open the door for you."

He said, "I understand."

I said, "If I open this door, I promise to God you better not try anything."

He said, "I won't. I promise."

I told him, "Walk out to the back road, so I can give you your wallet outside the back door."

I peeped out the back door and watched Darnell walk toward the alley. He had on some black boots, tan corduroy pants, a white turtleneck, a tan and dark brown sweater, and a black leather coat. I quickly unlocked the back door, swung it open, and sat his wallet on the closet pole next to my back door. I ran back in the house and locked the door.

He came back to the front door and knocked.

"What, Darnell?"

He replied, "Thank you. Can we please talk? I miss you."

I replied, "I don't know, but it is over between us." We did not talk that night, but slowly we started back talking again with him being on the other side of the door, until I felt comfortable talking to him with the door cracked, then with the door open, until I invited him back in.

It was a process, but he patiently and gracefully went through it. My body missed him, but I was not going to tell him that, or sleep with him. I invited him in while I was cooking dinner one day and asked if he wanted to have dinner with me. We talked until it was late. I knew he wanted to stay the night and I wanted him to stay the night too, but my heart was not ready. He grabbed his black leather coat off the back of my cream dining room chair effortlessly. We walked to the front door slowly and deliberately. He gave me a tight and warm hug. Both of us wanted to spend the night with each other after that embrace, but I told myself, "Don't be desperate or naive Eve. This same Darnell hurt you." He turned around slowly to leave. We said goodnight and I locked the door. Moments later I was kicking myself for not letting him stay.

There was a knock at the door, and I wanted it to be him. I opened the door ready to surrender, but dog-nabit it was my nosy neighbor Dana. "Hey girl I just saw Darnell leave." I flopped back down on the couch irritated that she was not him. She asked, "What he wanted?" I replied, "Nothing." She was talking, but my mind was somewhere else. After about twenty minutes of her talking, smelling like smoke, and fried chicken, I was too ready to tell her good night.

After she left, there was a knock on the door a couple minutes later. As I swung the door open, we smiled at each other. I started walking backwards pulling him by his jacket and shirt. He smiled. We cuddled on the couch, ignoring our hectic past and talked like old friends. The next morning, we smiled and walked toward the bus stop together, but he started slowing down, which was odd because he normally walked faster than I did. Heck, everybody walks faster than I do. When I looked around, he was slowing down and I could not miss my bus. I yelled, "I have to go." He nodded his head and waved his hand for me to keep going. I looked back a few minutes later, but I did not see him. I wondered where he went. That was weird.

The next day, we officially had a date night at my house. There was no way we were getting away from each other. He pulled me by my hands toward my bed. I paused and told him I am not ready yet. He said, "Ok." However, the desire was still there. He pulled the covers back and pulled me into the bed. Throwing his leg around me, he playfully started dry humping my leg. I squealed *NOOO* and laughed. He threw his arms around me, and held me. He whispered, "I am sorry. I missed you." I felt his wet warm tears on my back, as his long jet-black eyelashes tickled my back. I turned around to face him and told him, "I missed him too." I still chose not to sleep with him.

Weeks later, as we walked toward the bus stop the same thing happened, and I could not understand why he kept leaving me like that. I decided to go to my grandmother's house because I needed to figure out what was going on. I went home the next day, but I had decided not to see him any more until he was honest with me. It had been a month since I last saw him, and I was not about to let my guard down around him ever again.

 He knocked on the door one Saturday and I opened the door. I was nice and polite. We small talked for a while, but I was a different woman. I finished getting ready for work in front of him, not hiding my body from him. I oiled down my healthy plus size legs, and then I sat at the foot of the bed and slid my shoes on. Darnell got on one knee, grabbed my hand and asked, "Tanell, will you marry me?"

I laughed at him to his face. "Darnell, why would I marry you? You didn't treat me right when we were dating. I know you are not going to act right married. Thanks, Darnell, but I cannot marry you." I was thinking to myself that if he really wanted to marry me he would have showed me he loved and cared about me.

I am not a character in one of those Terri McMillan's books that is going to tolerate him acting a fool and pulling "Disappearing Acts," with me. I am pretty much done. As we got ready to leave, I paid close attention to him. I waited for him to pull his old "Disappearing Act." I acted as though I did not notice. I kept walking. When I looked back and did not see him, I ran to the corner of an apartment building, I passed daily on my way to the bus stop. I stood there and peeped around the corner and watched him go up to the second floor to the fourth apartment door.

I walked up the stairs, not fully knowing what I was going to see, or what would happen, but I just had to know. I knocked on the door and an African-American woman in her forties answered the door. She had a scarf on her head, and she had on a long-stripe-sleeveless-sundress. There were no smiles on our faces as we talked woman to woman, just understanding. Maybe she knew who I was, but I did not know who she was. When he saw me at the door, he jumped to his feet rushing towards me as if to stop me from causing a scene. It was too late. My last name was Allen, but Wright blood flowed through my veins. We are known to have quick tempers, to be bold and not allow anyone to put any fear in our hearts. I can honestly say that is not me unless I am severely provoked.

He knew he had better not "poke the bear." "What the hell, Darrnell! Who is this woman? Why are you at her house? Is this where you have been sneaking off to? Are you seeing her?"

I went down the steps firing questions. When I turned, I stepped on his foot. I could tell it hurt. Yet, it was nothing, compared to the punch and the push I gave him. He was tall and thin. Although, I weighed more than he did, he was a few inches taller than me. I began to cry in front of him for the first time. "I hate you; I knew I never should have given you another chance." I could see all the color draining out of his caramel colored face, his warm eyes glossed over with tears. "I never ever want to see you again." I marched off to the bus stop, freed by the truth and vowing never to give him another chance.

Dr. Maya Angelou, said, "When someone shows you who they are, believe them." If I stayed with him that would have meant I was choosing to turn a blind eye to the fact that he was not dependable, not good at communicating, or being honest. We were not dating when I followed him to that woman's house. I did not understand why he would propose to me knowing that he was seeing someone else. That is what hurt me, and the fact that he felt the need to be dishonest was the icing on the cake.

I did not see it as if he was cheating on me because we were not seeing each other in an intimate manner nor did we establish that we were getting back together. Note to self, if you do not set boundaries of what is or is not acceptable in a relationship, you're always going to have one party thinking it is okay to behave in any form or fashion.

Pearls of Wisdom

1. Both parties have to make sure they understand what a monogamous relationship is and if that is truly what they both want.
2. Set boundaries in the relationship to maintain mutual respect.
3. Develop safe words so that your partner knows when to cut off an argument. It will help make fighting fair and decrease chances of hitting below the belt in verbal arguments.
4. When you end a bad relationship, never go back thinking the person has changed if there has not been a time of reconciliation, healing, and significant change in behavior.
5. If you feel you have to resort to violence to express yourself, or you need to control your partner, this is a clear sign that this relationship is not for you.
6. If any form of abuse in the relationship occurs, seek professional help with law enforcement, anger management, and counseling.
7. Never give anyone permission to make you feel bad.

Chapter 7

My Muse

"You're my downfall, you're my muse. My worst distraction, my rhythm and blues..." -John Legend

I met My Muse while taking the Red line train to 95th Street and the Dan Ryan. I commuted back and forth from the Southside to the Northside of Chicago, where I attended Truman College, Technical Center. I noticed a pair of eyes watching me. They were warm, curious, and slightly shy. They belonged to a stranger on the train who wore simply a pair of jeans and a plain white T-shirt. When I looked up to see who they belonged to, the owner of them quickly and shyly looked away. As the doors opened, I heard the familiar sound of the conductor saying last stop 95th Street and the Dan Ryan.

I looked around for the stranger with the warm gaze who wanted to know more about me. I secretly wanted to know more about him, but he looked down at the ground as if he was not looking at me at all. I thought, maybe it was just in my head, *false alarm*. "The Stranger" was not checking for me after all. I asked myself, "Why would he be interested in me?" I did not have the greatest self-esteem at the time. I wanted him to come up to me and ask me for my phone number, but he never did.

One day, on that same train, while on my way to work, I saw "The Stranger," with the curious eyes. This time I told myself I was not going to let him get away. I looked at him and I said, "I know this sounds like a pick-up line, but I think I've seen you before, do I know you?"

My Muse said, "We exchanged numbers before."

I could not believe it. I must have been "chocolate wasted" if I gave this guy my number and I did not remember it. He was not the type of man you forgot, not with those eyes.

 He was beyond handsome with a beautiful-dreamy-shade-of-brown skin, and his curly Q-waves played neatly around his well-manicured hairline. He reminded me that we met one night on a train. It was very late and I was coming from school. I could not believe it; I must have been exhausted because I did not remember that we had met before.

My Muse said, "That's why I kept looking at you the other day, but you didn't remember me, so I didn't want to say anything."

He asked me, "How is school going? You really don't remember me, do you? You told me you had to make up hours and that you were in school to become a hairstylist. You were really tired and you told me not to try anything." I smiled as I said, "Ooooh!" It is funny because that sounds just like me, but to this day, I still don't remember meeting him.

My Muse did not have a phone, so he gave me his brother's number. Crazy names must have run in their family because his brother's name was weird too. I thought to myself this man is lying to me. In this day in time, who does not have a phone? He was telling the truth. It was always kind of late when I called with me working in a salon, which meant I always woke his brother up. As he hoarsely answered the phone, I always pictured him with skin the color of dark chocolate, this guy had to be attractive because he sounded dreamy even half asleep.

He was the first man that I felt without hesitation fully embraced my curves as a plus size woman. He openly welcomed and loved my stretch marks, fat rolls, and my double chin. He gladly grabbed my hand in public to let the world know we were together. Anytime I dared to mention losing weight, it was a form of blasphemy. He taught me never to be shy or ashamed of my body.

My Muse was unique and kind of odd. He was strange to most people who met him. My shampoo assistant TT met him and said, "That MF is crazy." I would have to agree he was rather odd, but I overlooked many things about him because I was in love with the idea of being in love and having a boyfriend.

He was a vegetarian and that was a new concept for me. This here is a straight "Meat-a-terian." I found myself bending one of my core rules about not dating men with children. He had a daughter. I thought it was crazy that he did not celebrate holidays because he was not a Jehovah's Witness or a Muslim. I often reminded him that his girlfriend celebrated all pagan holidays especially Christmas. He worked as a security guard, but he lived a step above paycheck to paycheck.

He was a very touchy-feely-man. He was the first man I slept with that I truly surrendered my body and my heart to leading to my first orgasm. The molestations that I experienced as a child did something to me mentally, emotionally, and physically. Even though I craved sex, I never relaxed enough to enjoy it. The trick to me surrendering was telling myself he was my husband. I knew then that I should not have been having sex outside of marriage. I also enjoyed sleeping with him because he was under the influence of a demonic puppet master manipulating his body to make me enjoy the fruit of our sin.

My Muse was very attentive to my needs as a woman. I knew he watched porn. We never watched it together, but I suspected that he was highly addicted to watching it and teetered on the line of being a "nympho." He often joked about wanting to become a porn star.

After we slept together, a couple days later he called me and broke up with me. During that conversation, it felt like something, or someone was playing with the strings of my heart. He was so indecisive and all over the place. I knew that even if we did get back together it would never be the same between us. He had proven to me that he could not be trusted with my heart, or my body.

We got back together, but it was brief. I wanted him to be the one, but he was not. Since I was a child, Holy Spirit has talked to me and I have had the gift of discernment, and the gift of the prophetic. I just did not know what it was called and I did not fully understand it then.

My Muse had a secret that Holy Spirit revealed to me, that I never realized. It was not until months later after we broke up and God was delivering me from the spirit of lust, that God showed me he suffered from severe depression. Holy Spirit told me if we had kids together, he would have molested them. I had to choose and think carefully about who allowed myself to like, to love, and to marry. I learned to pray and ask God to show me the spirit behind their face.

Every time we slept together, I was attacked by different spirits of self-loathing. This was because of the soul tie we had due to us having premarital sex. Most people never think about the spiritual, or emotional ramifications of having sex outside of marriage. One of the biggest issues is the forming of soul ties. They can be formed when we connect to people in intimate relationships by spending time with them, kissing, or having sex with them. These are usually unhealthy spiritual connections that are hard to break.

Looking back over my relationship with him, there were so many signs that we should not have been together. During this time in my life, I was desperate for love and attention, so I settled for an imitation of love, any form of affection, and attention I could get. I compromised many of my core values and standards for a man who could never truly love, value, appreciate, or minister to my spirit.

Pearls of Wisdom

1. You must learn to love yourself before you can ask anyone else to love you.
2. Exes are exes for a reason. Never go back with an ex unless you are sure this is God's divine will for your life.
3. Pray and ask God to break any soul ties that you may have that you are aware and unaware of existing.
4. Regardless of how someone looks, or behaves, always believe and trust Holy Spirit when He shows you who they really are, or what is going on with them.
5. Anytime you start dating, or you enter into a courtship with someone there needs to be some form of accountability by those who have your best interest at hand.

Chapter 8

Deliverance Has Come

"I need forgiveness for my sins, but I need also deliverance from the power of sin... I appreciate the blessed fact of God's forgiveness, but I want something more than that: I want deliverance. I need forgiveness for what I have done, but I need also deliverance from what I am."
- Watchman Nee

Ever since I was a child, I have operated in the gift of discernment. It is one of my strongest spiritual gifts, and it has saved my life many times while doing some dangerous and careless things. I got saved at a young age. I always knew I was different from most people, especially as a youth. As a kid, I prophesied to people in my family not fully knowing what I was doing. My family and I could see God's hand upon my life during my early childhood.

As I grew older, I began to look for love in all the wrong places. I stopped going to my church, which was a place that offered me so much freedom and growth. It was not intentionally. It started by me missing a Sunday here and a Sunday there. Spiritually I became weaker until the next thing I knew I had secretly become the promiscuous church girl next door engaging in risky behavior. Dating My Muse and Darnell slowed me down. I never cheated on them.

My Muse and I were planning to hook up over Easter weekend, but I had a major conflict. My Aunt Jewels and my Uncle Cedrick were pastors, and every Easter my family would go to support them and their ministry. I was not trying to go to church, especially since I had gotten in a habit of not going. I told my Auntie Meka, who was usually okay with me getting a social life outside of church that I was not going because I had plans.

She was like, "You on some other shit, have your ass ready to go to Jewels', Nell."

I whined, "Man, Auntie it is not going to start on time and My Muse and I are supposed to hook up this weekend."

My aunt is one of the smartest people I ever met, but there was no doubting Grandma Foxy was her momma. "Tell that nigga you will see him when you get back from church with your family, or else he can bring his ass too. Now what's the problem?"

I mumbled, "Nothing."

She said, "Good. Get your shit, and be ready when I come to get you tomorrow."

I felt like saying, "damn, damn, damn" in my Flora Evans voice from, "Good Times."

I was walking through my apartment about two weeks prior to Easter, and I heard Holy Spirit speak to me. "If you think he is good to you just wait until you meet who I have for you." I looked around the roomed puzzled not because God spoke to me because God has always spoken to me since I was a child in an audible voice, via discernment, or prophetically through dreams and visions. I was puzzled because even though I knew I was not living right God loved me, still desired to have a relationship with me, did not stop communicating with me, and wanted me to know that He had someone special for me and My Muse was not the one.

 I was eighteen when I questioned God for about a year about my purpose. "Why was I born God, and what am I supposed to be doing with my life?" I expected him to answer me right away in this, "Thou art God voice," and it never happened in that way. It was close to almost a year later. My family and I were in the Maryland DC area, to visit my Auntie Shay and her family. The snow was terrible that Christmas.

We were stuck in the house the entire time, except when we went to church. I was looking out the window and all I could see were blankets of beautiful white fluffy snow. I heard God speak to me in a quiet still voice. "Your purpose is to save souls and to draw as many souls to me as possible." I left Maryland knowing my purpose in life, but I would not have ever imagined in my wildest dream that God had called me to be a minister.

I called My Muse to delay our plans. I could not give him a specific time because my aunt and uncle had one of those doggone holy-roller churches that did too much. Even though I knew God worked through their ministry, I did not feel like spending my whole day in no doggone church. Every year it was the same mess. Beep-Beep! I put my coat on with an attitude vowing, next year I ain't going. I got into my Auntie's black two door Ford Explorer truck that I loved. As I got in, I tried to hide my disposition, but my Auntie never missed anything.

Although my Auntie Meka was only six years older than me, I knew not to play with her. She was the young, cool, hip auntie, but she did not allow us to disrespect her, or act a fool around her. She was never an absentee auntie. Yet, she did not play with us and we did not play with her. I saw her ram my cousin Sybil's head into my grandma's kitchen cabinets for stealing from our grandma and then lying to her about it. It does not make sense to argue with her because she was a wordsmith; you were not going to outthink her, or beat her in an argument. She should have been a lawyer instead of an educator.

I tucked my attitude in as I clicked on my seat belt.

She looked at me and said, "Good morning, what's wrong with you?"

I made sure I chose my words carefully. I said, "Nothing," as politely as I could.

She said, "Mmmhmm, you ain't feeling going to Jewels." Thank God, she said it and not me. I started laughing. She said, "I know, but sometimes you have to do what you have to do. That is life. We are only going for a few hours and then we will come back home."

I never knew God was setting me up to transform my life. My Aunt Jewels was a co-pastor, a prophet, a wife, a mother and an entrepreneur. She owned one of the most popular hair salons in the city of Elgin. She was light-skinned with hazel eyes. You could always tell what kind of mood she was in by looking at her eyes. She had been asking for a while if I wanted to do nails at her salon. I would always say, "Yes," but I never went. I was working at a good salon. I was not really feeling the commute all the way to Elgin, but I said yes.

I really had a good time at the Easter event with my family. My Aunt Jewels told my grandmother, "I don't think Nell is going to come, Momma." I really felt obligated to keep my word to prove her wrong. I told my friend Tia who I worked with about my auntie wanting me to do nails at her salon. Tia and I went to hair school together and she was one of the best stylists I ever met. We hit it off from the first day we met.

A number of girls we went to hair school with did not like her because she was so beautiful. They were jealous of her. They thought because she was so pretty and nicely dressed, she had to be conceited and stuck up acting, but she was not. She was one of the sweetest and humblest people I had ever met. She was very professional and hard working. Unlike mine, Tia's clientele took off like a wildfire as a stylist, not only was she an excellent hair stylist, she was extremely fast. Although, many of her male clients found her to be attractive, she never dated her clients, or flirted with them, unlike me.

She said, "Tanell, didn't Mrs. Baxter tell us not to date our clients. They are not going to want to pay you if you are sleeping with them."

"I know" I said with a smirk, "That's why I am going to stop doing his hair and keep sleeping with him."

She started laughing, "Girl, you are stupid."

I replied, "I know! Thank you very much!"

I told Tia about me taking the job at my aunt's salon a few days out of the week and she thought it was a bad idea. "Tanell you are not going to want to go way out there every week and come way back to the city. What about your apartment?"

I said, "I will live there three to four days out of the week."

She said, "Hell naaaw! Girl you are going to end up missing money, or quitting one of these salons because it is going to be too much for you. How are you going to get back and forth?"

I said, "I am going to take the train back and forth."

She said, "Girlll no! You are going to be super cold. Your aunt ain't going to give you a ride?"

I said, "I don't think so."

I do not know what it was about my Auntie Jewels' house, but it was different from any house that I ever visited. There was a peace that sucked you in. There was such a sweet spirit in her house that welcomed you there. I found myself in an arresting anointing there. I started getting to Elgin on Saturday nights, so I could go to church with them on Sunday mornings. I had never fully experienced services like that where people flowed in the prophetic and deliverance took place.

I loved staying at my aunt and uncle's house. You definitely could feel the presence of the Lord there. God would always wake me up in the wee hours of the morning. I would go in the bathroom and the Holy Spirit would just minister to me. God delivered me from lust in that bathroom. He told me not to date anybody for two years, not to give my number out, or sleep with anyone, and for forty days to fast from the time I woke up until noon, and to do the Daniel Fast. I only ate natural foods from the earth.

While dating My Muse I decided to go a month without eating meat, so my body was already detoxing from meat. I tried for a while to go back and forth to both salons before I eventually decided to quit my job in The City (Chicago), and to move in with my family in Elgin. God was leading me to move in with them so that I could begin my training for ministry.

It used to make me sick to my stomach when men tried to flirt with me after my deliverance from lust. My spirit was super sensitive and was able to discern any form of perversion. I did not allow any men to hug, or touch me. When the enemy would try to attack me in my sleep with the spirit of lust, my spirit man was so alert I would feel the spirit of God deflecting the spirit of lust where it could not even come near me.

In the early hours of the morning while I was meeting with Holy Spirit, He would unlock different mysteries in the Bible to me. One morning He told me about all of the spiritual gifts and talents that He placed inside of me. He told me I was a prophet. I remember being excited to share that with my aunt. When I told her, she said, "Mmm, I don't know about that." From that moment on I began to doubt who I was spiritually, and if God was talking to me. I stopped really knowing for sure if it was God, or me that was talking. After all, if my aunt and pastor could not confirm my gifting as a prophet, then I must have been off. I stopped telling people when I thought God was talking to me out of the fear of being wrong.

A couple of years later, my uncle and I went to visit one of his friend's churches, and it was rather interesting how one of the ladies was behaving. I did not say a word. After the service, my uncle and I were directed to the pastor's office.

He greeted us and inquired about the service. He and my uncle did the whole-male-church-pastor-lingo-doc-mess. Sitting there, I listened quietly.

The pastor then turned to me and asked me, "What did you see?"
I replied, "I didn't see anything." I thought to myself, "Oh no, I am not saying anything."

He, replied, "I don't know why you are saying that. You have a strong spirit of discernment, and not only that you are a prophet."

I looked at my uncle and he tilted his head to the side towards his friend giving me the okay to tell what I saw. When I finished, the pastor thanked me and told me I was on point and that God confirmed everything he had been feeling lately through me. I shared with my uncle what God told me about being a prophet and what happened when I told my auntie. He said, "Tanell, God may not always confirm your gifting through your leader, but that does not mean you're not called or anointed. God may not have showed them yet."

I became the singles minister a year after I started living a celibate and holy life. I began to make friends easily because of my bubbly personality. For the first time in my life, I believed that I was truly beautiful because I was a child of God. I decided to go through a purity ceremony to rededicate my body back to God. My aunt and uncle sat me down to talk to me about something important.

"Mocha, you have been doing really good with the singles ministry, and working on the finance committee, but we think you would also be great working with the youth." I added youth leader to my plate. I liked working with the youth and creating things for them to do.

Living with my aunt and uncle restored my hope in the Black family living in unity and Black love. I had never seen a couple so anointed as them. God would tell them the same thing in different parts of the city, state, and country. I felt loved and valued living with my aunt and uncle although money was often tight for us as a family of ten.

As an honorary pastor's kid (PK), I knew firsthand what most pastors' kids go through. You are always under a microscope for judgment. You should be the perfect example of everything because you are the pastors' kids, or you are stereotyped as being the worse kids.

Often, it is that pressure to behave or to perform a certain way that forces most PKs' to venture out to find their own identity. Oftentimes, you have to be the first people at the church and the last to leave. You have to pick up the many projects that everyone else drops, constantly giving, doing, and helping others.

I spent a great deal of time with my family. We worked together, went to church together, and lived together to the point sometimes things would spillover to other areas. My client Kendell began to notice a change in me. He and his wife Lillie were cool. I had been doing his hair for two-and-a-half years. They were like my older sister and brother. I would do Kendell's hair at 6:00 a.m. to get him in and out of the salon in a timely manner. He noticed the tension between my family and me when they arrived.

The next time I did his hair, he brought it up. "Mocha, I was talking to Lillie and told her that I could sense that you have been going through some things. My wife and I have been visiting a new ministry, and I would like to invite you to join us. I would have invited you sooner, but I did not want to step on anybody's toes. Mocha, my wife and I love you, and we are not going to let you die spiritually."

I started crying because he was telling the truth. I loved my family, but it was time for us to go our separate ways so we all could be who God had called and created us to be.

I was starting to die spiritually because I had no place to escape where I could be me. I had been attending college for almost a year. I decided it was time for me to move out of my family's house, and it helped our relationship tremendously. I went to Bible study at this small ministry called "House of Hope" that Lillie and Kendell invited me to. It was nice, but I thought it was kind-of-corny and something was missing. I never would have thought in a million years that I was what was missing from the ministry.

I enjoyed going to Bible study with them. Less than a month later, my uncle released everyone in the ministry in Elgin and in Carpentersville to House of Hope. My uncle told me we were going to talk about something later that week, but when I went to Bible study, Pastor Jay told me "You have been released into your destiny." From that day forth, my life and ministry have never been the same.

I soon stopped working in my family salon for personal reasons. I simply felt like the best thing for me to do at that time was to separate myself peacefully from my family. For almost two years, I did not talk to them. House of Hope and my friends became my family.

Eventually, we started talking again and things began to get better between us. They were very proud, supportive, and affirming of me getting accepted to Spelman College. By this time, I was getting ready to move down South to attend college. I had been at House of Hope for over three years. All of my friends attended House of Hope because I invited them; however, Holy Spirit drew them. House of Hope was so different. It was a great church; you could just feel the love as you walked through the doors. Our pastors wanted us to be successful in every aspect of our lives. They were supportive of my collegial and personal goals.

I took the vision seriously, to allow God to heal and mend me in every aspect of my life. My pastors illustrated to me on a daily basis that every great leader had to learn the art of serving first. My pastor and I became very close; he became a father figure and mentor to me. I got along with both of my pastors very well. I could always be honest with them.

My friends tried to convince me that I should not be on the party line talking to guys. I paid them no attention with their Sister-Christian-looking-selves. I said, "I don't see anything wrong with it, and I am going to keep on doing it unless God says something different."

One of them was like, "I bet you won't tell Pastor Jay that you be on there!"

I grabbed my cell phone and dialed his number in front of both of them.

"Hello," his rich professional voice poured through the speaker.

I heard that in high school, he had been a smart jock. I never pictured him as anything other than Pastor Jay, an entrepreneur, husband to Faith, community leader, and a father figure. I strongly resented anybody trying to tell me anything differently.

I told him about me talking to guys on the party line. He was honest and nonjudgmental. He actually gave me great advice. He warned me to be careful, and not to share my personal information with people online. He often gave me the type of advice that a father would give to his daughter. They covered me spiritually and sent me away to college to pursue my goals and dreams. Every chance I got, I returned to House of Hope, the place that was home for me spiritually.

Pearls of Wisdom

1. Deliverance requires total obedience to God.
2. Change is necessary for true growth.
3. True friends will be honest with you, even if they have to step on your feelings or the feelings of others.
4. Family will not always be biologically related to you.
5. Never allow unforgiveness to fester.
6. "Unforgiveness is like drinking poison and waiting for your enemy to die."
7. It is okay to be the first person to apologize.
8. Strongholds are broken through fasting and prayer.
9. Never burn bridges in relationships and friendships; always try to leave on good terms.

Confessions of a Lost Sheep

Chapter 9

Saving Grace

"Our worst days are never so bad that you are beyond the reach of God's grace. And your best days are never so good that you are beyond the need of God's grace"
-Jerry Bridges

I was tired of long-distance relationships and dating "Randoms" off the party line and online. Some plus size people hide or turn to online dating because of their size. I dated online because socially I was able to meet more people and felt less awkward.

I have never had much of a social life outside of church and my friends from there. Some of my cousins down South labeled me as a "church girl." Online I was able to have my own personality outside of church. Yet who I truly was always seemed to seep through my online persona, creating tiredness in me because I was often trying to be someone I was not.

I was talking to this real yellow lemon head looking dude, that I met on the party line. He was the biggest liar I had ever seen on this side of heaven. I had had enough of his mellow-yellow mess. In the words of My Bestie, Ms. Priss-priss, My Spelman Sister – Courtney voice, "GIRLLL, this negro has gotten on my last nerve!"

She always made me laugh or smile at how she said the word "negro." Courtney had a classy style about her. When she walked into a room, she flowed into it gracefully and elegantly. She had a presence about her that made most men think that she would be great wife material.

"Negro" was not the only word that made me laugh at her. She also had a way of saying "dammmn!" Her beautiful locks, *cocolicious* skin-tone, and her stunning resemblance to Issa from the HBO hit sitcom *Insecure*, gets her stopped all the time.

In my Courtney voice, I found myself saying, "I'm sick of this negro. He ain't adding nothing to me, so I need to do the subtracting. I am so over this party line dating."

Atlanta is so different from Chicago. Anytime I went to Chicago, "The City," compared to the western suburbs of Elgin and Carpentersville, guys would always ask for my number, or try to talk to me, but not in the ATL, or at Spelman. Nobody was checking for me. I was like, "God, where is my *Spelhouse* romance in the making at? You do know a Spelman Woman + a Man of Morehouse = *Spelhouses*. Why can't I meet someone the old-fashioned way, the way they do in those Hallmark movies? The next guy I date; I am going to meet him the old fashioned way. I am just going to bump into him. I am so done with this party line mess."

This is a perfect example of why we have to be so careful about what we say. In my frustration, I openly declared how I was going to meet my next boyfriend. That very same day I met Winston while walking on the sidewalk to Spelman, coming from Jasmine's Café. I saw a tall, brown-skinned attractive, athletic man watching me. I could not understand why he was staring at me so hard.

I asked him, "Why are you staring at me so hard?"

He said, "I don't know; I might see something I like."

I said, "I know you heard it's not polite to stare."

Something about this guy seemed a little strange. Since I could not put my finger on it, I thought maybe he was just socially awkward. We started small talking and he asked, me "What is your name?"

After we did the polite introductions of ourselves, I learned that his name was Winston. He worked at Morehouse College in the cafeteria, but his dream was to become a pilot. I could see him being a pilot. He asked if I had a man and I shyly replied, "No." I do not know why I was so embarrassed to admit to him that I did not have a man. I guess because the last guy I liked in the AUC did not really like me like that. The truth is, at the time, I was struggling with my self-confidence in meeting guys in Atlanta.

He asked me for my phone number and I told him no. I had just said before I left my house the next person I date I was going to meet them the old-fashioned way maybe bump into them while shopping--Can you believe it? I bumped into him. I only said no to giving him my number because I could not afford to get distracted right now. I had to make sure I did what I needed to do to graduate. We said our goodbyes and walked away from each other, probably thinking that we would never see each other again.

I song on the AUC praise team and we had just finished singing on Morehouse campus. I was feeling the spirit and the power of God all over me. I felt rejuvenated and ready to strike out running spiritually and naturally. I wanted to hang out at Jasmine's with my friends, and check out the poets. It was a warm spring night, and I really did not want to do any homework, but I heard Holy Spirit tell me to go straight home; do not stop.

While walking on the Morehouse campus to cut across to get home, I heard a familiar voice say, "Hello."

I turned to see who had spoken to me. It was the shy awkward pilot-to-be who asked for my phone number.

He smiled at me and asked me, "How are you doing tonight?"

I replied, "Blessed." Not lessening my stride.

He asked, "What are you about to do?"

I said, "Go home and study. I'm really busy right now. I'm trying to finish my senior thesis."

He said, "Are you too busy to have dinner with me, or for me to take you out for coffee one day?"

I smiled slightly trying to give the brother a winning chance. I thought, "Boy this man does not waste any time. This is his second time he has seen me and he is already trying to ask me out on a date. I did not give him my phone number, and he still has the confidence to ask me out on a date. This dude is persistent."

As we walked and talked, I found out a little bit more about him. He had kids, and I don't mean one or two kids. He had kids, too many for me to count. I smiled at him when he told me he had kids and how many he had because this has really sealed his fate with never dating me. I do not date divorcees and men with kids. If you lie to me about being divorced or having kids, when I find out, I am going to break up with you because you were being deceitful.

I said, "I am not trying to be funny, but I do not date guys with kids." He was so humble and sweet; I did not really know how to take him.

He said, "I hope you won't hold my children against my future with you."

I looked away not sure what to say. I would hate the fact that somebody chose not to date my sister because she had two kids, but I just never liked the idea of dealing with "baby mama drama" or my husband having children with another woman. It may seem selfish in this day and age, but I have always pictured my husband and me enjoying the experience of us having children for the first time together. I smiled and kind of laughed lightheartedly.

He asked, "Have you eaten?"

I said, "No."

He said, "I'm on my way to work and I could make you some dinner."

I said, "I am not really sure about that. I really need to be getting home. I have a lot of homework that I need to finish."

I wondered to myself what if this is just what I have been praying for, and I was just being too foolish to recognize it, while it was standing right before me. I told God and myself that I wanted to meet somebody the old-fashioned way, just bump into them.

Wow, I literally bumped into him. I am not sure how to respond. You know Nelly-Nell "love the kids," but I ain't trying to be nobody's step-momma. Look at me, this is only my second time seeing him and I am already planning our lives together.

I told myself "Girlll, get a grip! He just wants to feed you! What the Dickens! I am doing it again. I am always over thinking, always over-analyzing, and always looking two to three years ahead in the future. STOP! Chill, relax, and enjoy the moment. Girl, you are only 30, so what if I am older than most of my Spelman sisters and one girl calls me Ms. Tanell!"

For some funny reason I was enjoying strolling through the campus of Morehouse with him; talking, smiling, and enjoying his companionship. To be honest, I did not want the night to end, but I knew I needed to get home.

He really was speaking my language, "the way to my heart is through my stomach, amen."

As we made it to the front of Kilgore, where he worked on Morehouse campus, he said, "Give me one minute! Let me go check in."

As soon as he disappeared through the doors, I pulled out my cell phone and I heard the familiar voice of my friend Smitty.

"Heeey Nelll."

 I said, "Hey Smitty. I need your advice; I met this nice guy. He wants to make dinner for me at his job, but I don't know. I am somewhat scared. I don't really know what to do."

She said, "Well, it could not hurt to go to dinner with the guy. You said he is a nice guy. You will never know until you try."

"I don't know Smitty. He has too many kids. I just don't date men with kids."

Smitty said, "What if this is who God has for you and you let the fact that he has kids stop you from meeting him; and also, Nell you are just going to dinner with him. You don't even know if you would like him enough to want to marry him. Just go to dinner and maybe have a good time and see where it goes from there. That is what being single is all about, trying stuff out to see if it works for you. You are in college. Have a good time."

I said, "Thanks Smitty."
She said, "You are welcome. Have a good time and call me tomorrow to tell me how the date went."

As I hung up the phone, I smiled to myself.

Winston came out smiling at me. "So, are you going to let me make dinner for you tonight?"

I shyly said, "I guess."

He let me into the formal dining room of Morehouse and it was so beautiful. It seemed so dark and romantic with clear Christmas lights hanging. He sat me at a table by myself in a completely empty room and he told me "I will be right back."

He constantly came back and forth to check on me to bring me food and occasionally slow dance with me on the carpeted floor of the dining hall. I guess you could say that our first date was very romantic and whimsical. It was almost like magic. For some reason, I knew it was a date I would never forget.

I stayed with him his entire shift. The sun was getting ready to come up when we left. We went to my house and, as we walked there, I was like maybe we should just go get coffee and donuts.

He said, "Maybe I can take you on a date tomorrow; I'm kind of tired."

A part of me felt reluctant to have him come over to my house so soon, but the other half felt like, he just worked all night; while he sleeps you can study. I do not think either one of us got any sleep because we talked and got to know each other better. We got involved in a full-fledged relationship very quickly without taking the time to really get to know one another intimately. Of course, we knew each other's best representatives by asking each other questions and knew superficial stuff about each other.

I am talking about knowing each other because we have spent time together learning, growing, and bonding with each other through life's situations. It was almost as though we were caught up in a whirlwind. We felt very comfortable with each other. In a very short period, we were doing pretty much everything together.

He worked at Kilgore, right at the back foot of Morehouse campus, before walking up the hill to Purdue, which was down the hill from the house where I rented a room. He always took time to cater to me, and he was extra nice to my friends. My friend Amelie liked him from the first day she met him. Whenever, I did her hair, he brought food that she could eat because she was vegetarian. She always asked, "Where's Win at?"

OMG! Winston trusted me with everything. I remember the first time he trusted me to cut his hair and the guard fell off the clippers; it was not funny. I felt so bad I had to cut all his hair off and give him a hard lining. He tried to cheer me up, but I felt so embarrassed as a hair stylist for jacking up his haircut.

He said, "It looks nice. It is just short. It is okay, my hair grows quickly. It will grow back."

Everyone who met Win liked him. I met a woman who he went to school with that worked at Spelman and she said, "You got yourself a good man; he's nice, he's really smart, kind-of-quiet, and hard working. You two will do well together."

I smiled because that is just what I wanted to hear, "we would do well together."

I went by Winston's job on my way home.

He told me, "I am tired. I am going to come over after I get off to get some rest."

I said, "No problem, knock on my window and I'll let you in the back door."   I do not know why, but for some reason I never heard Winston knocking at my window and I am a light sleeper. My roommates said he knocked at the door a few times, but they didn't let him in because when he knocked on the window I didn't open the door, so they assumed that I did not want him to come in.

I lived in a huge duplex house. I had seven roommates who lived in a separate apartment up above me and six housemates who lived in the same house with me. Each apartment had 7 bedrooms and two bathrooms, for seven college women to rent. It was two days later before I would hear from Winston, and I was pissed. I did not understand why he would not communicate with me for two days. I was not about to allow this to go on in this relationship.

If he is not going to do something, he needs to call and let me know. We were supposed to go to church together that weekend, but he never showed up. I don't know what's going on with him, but I am going to get to the bottom of this. I am going to put my foot down. I don't know who he thinks he is, but this foolishness is not going to happen with me again.

When we spoke, I asked him," Where have you been, and why haven't I heard from you?"

He said, "I have been keeping something from you that I need to let you know about. Sometimes, if I don't take my medicine like I'm supposed to, and I have seizures."

It felt like my heart stopped. I know a little about seizures, due to my uncle and my cousin Shae having them. They scared the dickens out of me.

"Winston, I'm sorry you didn't feel well, but how am I supposed to know that you have seizures, if you don't tell me? It is still not acceptable for you to be missing in action. If something is going on you need to let me know. What if you had a seizure and no one was around to get you the medical help you needed? You still need to let people know what is going on with you."

He gave me a hug and some playful kisses to the forehead and said, "I'm sorry Babe."

I left Winston in my room resting, while I went about running errands on campus. When I came home, he was standing on the porch. My roommate Justice was naturally beautiful with brown *coco-licious* skin and a head full of wavy-curly-2B-hair with a slight reddish-brown tint on the ends of it. That deceived most people into thinking it was her natural hair. I knew better because since she moved from Cali to the ATL, I had been her hair stylist. She and four of my other housemates went to Clark Atlanta, while CeCe and I went to Spelman.

She said, "Tanell, while you were gone your boyfriend was standing in the doorway watching us like a pedophile.
I don't know, something about him made me uncomfortable."

I neither confirmed nor denied what my roommate said. However, I tucked it into my spirit and prayed about it.

I never told anyone about the way he joked around with me a few times.

He said, "I'm going to take you to my house and tie you up, rape you, and have my way with you. You belong to me."

For some reason, when he would say that, I would always say, "The Devil is a Lie! You are not going to do anything to me."

Although, he had only said it three times, he had said it enough to make me wonder every now and again if it was safe for me to visit his house. I remember the first and only time I went to his house. I grabbed my razor off my dresser; I had just used to arch my eyebrows and said, "I wonder should I take this?"

He jumped back and said, "What do you need a razor for?"

I said, "You are right. I don't need it." When he left out the room, I wrapped the razor inside of a piece of paper towel and stuck it in my bra. For some reason, my stomach felt weird and fluttery. I called my sister as well as Pastor Faith to let them know my whereabouts, and I told my sister that I would let her know when I got there safely. I also made them aware that I would call them in the morning to let them know I was okay.

 I do not know what was going on with my stomach, but as soon as we got on the first bus, I suddenly had to poop. We had to take two buses and a train to get to his house. I thought several times for sure I was going to crap my pants. He gently held my hands and placed his head to my forehead while talking me through not having an accident in public. He was so sweet, nurturing, and caring towards me. I let go all of the bad thoughts. A person who showed so much love and care towards me would never do anything to hurt me.

After, I came out of the bathroom, I began to look around Win's apartment. I began to see little things that belonged to me like hand decorative towels and my house shoes. He never took anything major like my credit cards, my social security card, or money because every time I left him there I always checked for major things like that, but I never checked for hand towels and house shoes. I never really missed them to be honest until I saw them.

I was extremely upset because I felt like if he would take little things like that from me, what else would he take without asking. If we are supposed to be in a relationship and he cared about me why would he take from me?

When I confronted him about it, he said, "I didn't think it was a big deal. I didn't think you would mind."

I said, "But I mind because you did not ask me and you just took them from my house."

He apologized and began to rub my back. "I'm sorry Baby. I didn't mean to make you uncomfortable. I would never do anything to hurt you. You're my partner and my lover."

It is funny because for the first time Winston and I slept in a bed without being intimate or being too close to one another.

I prayed for God's divine hedge of protection around me that night. For some reason, there was nothing but space and opportunity between the two of us as we slept on his air mattress. The next morning, I asked, "Why did you sleep so far away from me? Are you mad at me?"

He said, "No, I just knew you were tired and I was allowing you to rest. I knew you needed to be up early for class this morning." He went to the store to grab a couple items to make me a junk food breakfast that consisted of Coca-Cola and two honey buns. After breakfast, we commuted to Spelman.

As we waited at the bus stop in the West End for the AUC shuttle to take me to campus, two guys walked by and were checking me out. I smiled and acted as if I did not notice, focusing on Winston's face as he smiled knowing that I was simply his lady. He stepped a bit closer to me, wrapping his arms around my waist and pulling me closer to him.

I smiled as we played around and waited for the shuttle. The shuttle was taking too long, so we decided to walk to campus. By this time, I was slightly running late for my Spanish class, "No hablo Español." My Spanish class was a beast to deal with all within itself. I needed to be on time for that class, a sister was already struggling.

He kissed me and told me, "I will see you later tonight."

I waited for him, but he never came. I never got a call or text to reassure me that he was okay. One day, two days, three days passed. By the end of the third day, I was ready to send a search party out to look for him. I was afraid that he had had a seizure. All kinds of thoughts ran through my head; what if no one was there to help him? What if he had died? I called his job and they said, "He has not been here."

On the 4th day, he called me and told me, "I had a very bad seizure and I have been in the hospital. I am feeling better now. I wanted to call you, Baby, to let you know I was okay."

I was so relieved that he was better.

He said, "I'll come by and see you after work."

After that, it was as if Winston was his self again.

We started spending a lot of time together and working on things as if nothing had ever happened. I was rushing to get ready for Founders Day. I was putting on my white dress and my black heels. I quickly grabbed my tote housing my senior project with all of my research in it that I was going to be speaking on and presenting to the religious studies committee. When I snatched my tote off the floor, it ripped, causing the strap on it to pop.

I was so disappointed. It was not just any tote. It was my favorite because it was very sentimental to me. My Spelman Sister and friend, Lexi Pooh, gave it to me for my birthday. I loved it. The cover had Phillis Wheatley quilted on it. Both of our birthdays are in January, and this was the first gift she ever gave me to symbolize our sisterhood and friendship.

I was so excited to go to Founders Day with Winston by my side supporting and cheering me on. Founders Day is a big deal at most Historical Black Colleges and Universities, especially at Spelman. We worked hard to celebrate the day by wearing white dresses, black shoes, skin tone stockings and no jewelry except a watch. It is supposed to be symbolic in representing our ancestors who went before us and wore their best. They did not have the luxury of having different accessories.

As I lined up next to my Spelman Sisters, I saw a new face, someone I had never met before. Her name was Kendra. She was beautiful and a plus size woman like me. I felt as though I had met a kindred spirit and found a new friend in my Spelman Sister. As we small-talked and got to know each other better, I learned that she was married. Her husband was an IT person, and they had no kids yet. I was so excited! I told her about Winston and that maybe we should get together and double date. She enjoyed the idea and she was looking forward to it.

After the celebration ceremony in Sisters Chapel for Founders Day, I excused myself from Kendra and Win, leaving them standing there next to each other. I went upstairs mainly to use the restroom right across from the cafeteria. As I came out of the stall to wash my hands, I looked up in the mirror and I saw Kendra standing there. She looked as if she was terrified.

I asked her, "What's wrong?" She looked as if she had seen a ghost. Something obviously frightened her.

I asked her several times, "What's wrong? What happened? Are you okay?"

She shook her head "yes," but I could not get her to tell me the truth. I tried to convince her to come eat lunch with us, and she shook her head violently "no."

When I went outside, I asked, "Winston what happened to Kendra? What's wrong with her?"

He assured me, "I don't know. She just went upstairs."

He surprised me with a beautiful new tote to replace the one I had broken that morning. He began to transition the items in my broken tote into my brand new one, and neatly folded up my old tote and placed it inside my new one.

As Winston and I walked away, I noticed one of the younger African-American ladies that worked in the cafeteria watching us very closely. We went downstairs and had lunch at the grill on Spelman's campus. I could not help but to be slightly distracted wondering about my new friend, who seemed visibly shaken up for some reason.

After, lunch I walked with Winston to the bus stop in front of Manley and a group of girls ran by. Some of them were wearing short-shorts and t-shirts.

I said, "Go ahead, you can look."

He said, "No, I see everything I want right in front of me."

I smiled, and I said, "Mmmmmhhhhhmmmm!"

He said, "Come on, don't you want to go home with me?"

I shook my head no. "I want to, but I cannot. I have too much work to do. I have to finish this proposal to submit to the committee, or I won't graduate on time."

He had something in his pocket that he kept fidgeting with and determination in his eyes, but I was not budging.

He said, "Let me use your cell phone. This detective left her card on my door and I want to call to see what she wants."

He called the detective from my phone, but she did not pick up. A few hours later, an unfamiliar number called my phone. I answered, "Hello!"

The detective introduced herself and asked if she could speak to Winston because he had left a message identifying who he was. I said, "He's not available right now. Can I have him call you back?"

She said, "Please do, it's very important that I speak with him as soon as possible."

Two days passed by and I had not spoken to Winston again. I said to him, "That detective that you called the day before yesterday called you back twice."

I told him, that I told her, "I'm sorry he's not available. I'm his girlfriend. Is there a message that you would like me to give him?"

She replied, "No, please just have him call me as soon as possible. It's very important I speak to him."

I began to wonder why it was so important for this woman to speak with him. That night I had a dream that he had raped my roommate, Justice. When I woke up, I called my best friend Eve and told her what had happened in the dream. I also told her about the detective that kept calling for him.

I said, "I wondered how people are married to serial killers and murderers, and they never know anything about it."

She said, "Yeah, girl, I wonder that too. That is a person who lives a double life.'

I said, "Maybe they are like a Dr. Jekyll and Mr. Hyde." All I know was something was going on with Win, and I wanted to get to the bottom of it.

The next day when Winston and I were hanging out, I told him about the detective calling for him. He called her back, but it was as if they were playing the worst case of phone tag. They never seemed to catch one another at the right time. I went to lunch a little later that day, and I saw the lady in the cafeteria who had been watching me and Winston talking one day.

She said, "*Comm'mere.*"

I said, "Yes?"

She said, "You go with that man I saw you with?"

I said, "Yes, Winston is my boyfriend."

She said, "I'm going to tell you this: you need to leave him alone. He is crazy and he got a lot of kids. He has been in jail before. I saw him down the street yelling one time. His momma lives by me. You got too much going for yourself to get mixed up with him."

This was the first time I had ever heard anybody ever say anything negative about Winston. To my knowledge, everybody loved him and spoke highly of him; classmates, coworkers, friends, hell, even my friends liked him.

No one once ever said a negative word about him. Who was she to try to change my mind about my boyfriend based on what she saw or thought she saw? I replied, "Really? Thank you for letting me know, but I never heard anyone say a negative word about Win. Thank you again, I needed to know this." I tucked it away in the back of my mind.

By the third call, the detective had grown irritated and impatient with playing phone tag with Winston. I could tell she was trying her best to be professional and patient; yet, she seemed sick of him.

I said, "Can I ask what this is regarding, that he needs to call you back?"

She replied, "No ma'am I cannot discuss that with you."

I said, "Okay, I will have Winston call you tomorrow when he gets in."

Something in my spirit would not let this go. I called her back two minutes later. I said, "I know you cannot tell me what this is pertaining to, but my parents sent me away to Spelman to go to school. I would like to know, if I was your daughter, would you want somebody like Winston dating your daughter?"

She replied, "No ma'am!"

I said, "Thank you, have a great night," and hung up the phone in disbelief. I did not sleep well that night. I prayed, and I commanded my body to rest in Jesus' Name. The next day was very busy for me. I could not focus on all this nonsense with Winston. I had to get my work done. That day Winston came over and we hung out.

I stressed to him the importance of him getting in touch with the detective. He walked me to praise team practice as he held the umbrella over my head, so I would not get wet in the rain. He told me he would be there promptly to pick me up when practice was over, but he left the umbrella with me. I gave him my cell phone to use to call the detective back as I went inside the little small Chapel on Morehouse campus to have praise team practice.

It ended slightly early, so I began to walk home. Winston was walking toward me in the rain. He kissed me on the cheek when he reached me. He told me he spoke to the detective and gave me my phone back. He told me, "If the detective calls back, describe to them what I am wearing. Tell them I am getting on the train to meet them at the station for questioning and speak with them about the case that they asked me about."

He gave me his wallet, and told me to order groceries. He told me he would be back as soon as possible. They just wanted him to come down to the station to answer some questions. When the detective called back moments later, I told her everything he told me to tell her.

She said, "No ma'am he will not be back; he's being charged with two counts of rape and kidnapping."

I could barely talk. I hoarsely said, "WHAT?" Justice's words, the young woman from the cafeteria, and the detective's words came rushing back to me.

All I could think of were pedophile, crazy, raping, tying up, and kidnapping. I felt as if the room was spinning, and someone was playing a cruel joke on me. How could the same person who is so loving and tender towards me be a monster?

I thought about the times I dismissed him saying, "I am going to take you to my apartment, tie you up, rape you, and have my way with you."

Now that I was thinking clearly, I asked myself what kind of normal or sane person jokes about raping someone. Yes, I know he took my personal belongings, but I did not think he was taking away women's rights and ability to choose if they wanted to have sex with him.

I could not help but think that all of those times he was missing in action he was out raping and kidnapping women while I was sitting around here like a damn fool, "acting like he was the best thing since sliced bread."

I cannot even imagine what he said or did to Kendra. I could not believe that the same day he tried to get me to go home with him he raped someone. I wondered what he would have done to me if he had me alone at his house.

She replied, "Ms. Allen, we need you to come down to the station for questioning. We need a statement from you."

She called several times, but I could not; I just could not do it.

If it had not been for God, my sister, and my pastors, I would have lost my mind and flunked out of college. It was the first time I felt like I could not call my pastor; he was not the one I needed. I needed my other pastor; his better half. I told her everything that happened, and she began to minister to me and pray for me, but most of all she covered me. I knew she would relay everything that happened to him, but I just could not tell him. I told my pastor about a few things when he called to check up on me a few days later.

"I am not going to ask you to re-live that, but that guy did not try anything with you, did he; because I will get my bat."

I said, "No," with a slight smile. It was my first smile since everything unfolded.

The negative stigma of his crime coupled with my poor choices in men left me feeling ashamed and embarrassed. I felt utterly humiliated. I had to get tested for STDs and deal with the whispers and the stares of people until I refused to allow them to make me or hold me accountable for the things that he did.

I remember walking into the cafeteria of Morehouse while I was in the summer intensive Spanish program, not wanting to eat there because those same co-workers, that he introduced me to knew what he had done, and knew I was his girlfriend. The incident had me questioning what I did wrong as a woman. Even though we were not married, we were sleeping together. I knew I should not have been sleeping with him, but did it to cater to him. It made me question what about my body and my sexuality was not fulfilling enough for him, that he felt he had to rape these women, force them to sleep with him by tying them up and holding them hostage in his apartment.

 I had to deal with the guilt of me putting my housemates and my Spelman Sisters in danger until I refused to continue to allow myself to take responsibility for his ill-mannered actions.

I never went to see him. He never called me, not even collect. I would have never taken a call from him, so I was glad that he never reached out to me. I was done with him when I found out that he was charged with two counts of rape and kidnapping. That is someone I did not want to have a future with and I sure as hell was not going to go see him or help him.

Due to the stress and trauma, I threw myself into my work. I made time to go by the clinic on campus to get tested for STDs; however, I never took time to get the results from the test. A part of me was fearful of going back to get the results. I did not find out the results of the test until later that summer.

Thank God, I was HIV-negative. However, I tested positive for chlamydia. Out of all the risky and promiscuous behavior I did in the past, I never got pregnant or contracted a STD, but the one time I slept with someone after choosing not to have sex again until I am married I did. I was super embarrassed. I shared with my sister what happened, she said, "Thank God Nell, it could have been worse. It could have been something you could not have gotten rid of.   That can come from wiping with the wrong tissue; that is not major. Get you some penicillin. It is going to clear that right up. You're going to be all right." I thought to myself, what if I am not all right? This has been a lot to take in all at one time.

While working at my church in Chicago, I told my pastor what happened. He was very supportive and he made sure I got my medicine. I do not know what I would have done in this case without God's grace, my pastors and my sister. They refused to allow me to drop the ball.

Pearls of Wisdom

1. Be careful what you speak out of your mouth because Satan hears just like God does.
2. Always follow God's instructions to the fullest when He tells you to do something.
3. In the words of the late Dr. Maya Angelou: "When someone shows you who they are believe them."
4. Any time you start liking, dating, or courting someone, you need to allow others in your intimate circle of accountability partners know so they can check that person out. They may see something you do not see.
5. Do not talk to (date) or bring home every stray person that pursues you or says they like you.
6. Do not dismiss the red flags you discern, see, or hear.
7. Never take on guilt from other people's bad choices and actions that have nothing to do with you.

Chapter 10

Looking for Mr. Right, but Settling for Mr. Wrong

"I have certain standards for myself so if something drops beneath that standard or if the opportunity doesn't fit who I am authentically at my core - I don't invest time where my brand isn't respected or where what I have to offer isn't appreciated." - **Bishop T.D. Jakes**

"Bad, bad, bad, bad, boys, make you feel so good, make you feel so good!" My bestie Eve and I had been talking on the phone since I left for Spelman. I really missed her at times and I was terribly homesick. Eve had just gotten into a new relationship, and she was head over heels in love with the guy. Spring break was rapidly approaching, and I was excited about going to visit Duke University.

I was trying to figure out how I was going to be able to do a college tour for graduate school when we came up with a solution. Eve would fly to Atlanta; we would rent a car and drive to South Carolina and North Carolina. The more I thought about it, the more it seemed like a great idea. We would get to spend some quality time together while road tripping. I would be able to see Duke with my friend, and she would get to see her new man.

I had no idea that the new man was in "cell block eight." Chris was white, and he definitely had her heart and nose wide open. Eve rented a nice white car. It looked like a Charger; I loved riding down the streets with the music booming in the AUC. I felt like, man, finally, I am an adult. Oh, you know it is sad, but it's serious, you are looking at someone who did not get their driving license until they were 28 years old, so to drive through the AUC with the music pumping while the wind was blowing through my hair was a good experience for me.

I was so excited to see Duke. I had been excited ever since the recruiters came to Spelman and sold me on it. I remember it as if it was yesterday. It was an African-American woman, and this white lady named Sari. Sari was so passionate when she described her experience of attending Duke, it just pulled on my heartstrings. I loved our girls' trip. We listened to music and had a great time. Eve did most of the driving because we did not trust my driving skills on the expressway since I was a new driver. As she talked to the love of her life, he had a friend that they wanted to introduce to me. I was not riding, walking, skipping, or hopping with excitement.

I know how those men in jail think. I told her she was not going to hook me up with somebody in the penal system. Unlike Eve, I had brothers, uncles, and cousins who had been incarcerated; I knew the song and dance they did while in prison.

They would have different girls writing them to keep them company, promising them the world and when they got out, they did a U-turn. No, thank you. You would not hook me up with a felon. In addition, I knew I was too good for anybody in the prison system; not trying to be arrogant or anything, but what could they do for me in prison? For me to date them would be me dating down. I told her several times I did not want to talk to him, but she ended up putting me on the phone with him.

I was so rude to this guy *the* Holy Spirit in me was offended on every level. He said, "Hey how are you doing. My name is Eric."

I said, "**WHAT**," with as much attitude as I could muster up. You could just hear the ignorance dripping in my voice. I was extremely rude as he tried to have a conversation with me. I did not want to be bothered with him, and that we were not on the same level.

I heard him tell his friend, "Here man, get this phone. This girl is rude as hell."

I guess it did not sit so well with our friends. Eve scolded me for acting *saddidy*. On top of that, Holy Spirit was convicting me too. Later that night, I apologized to him for being extremely rude. I asked him to please, forgive me.

He said, "Okay. A lot of women have been wrong about what they think about men in prison. They think because a man is in prison, they are desperate to be with a woman. I'm not desperate and you did not have to be rude."

I apologized again hoping that I could, I mean we could start over. I told myself I would be politer to him, but let's face it I'm not interested in dating him. However, he did give me a blow to my ego, when he said, "Men in prison are not desperate for a woman."

I sat and thought briefly for a moment about my own brothers who had been incarcerated, my uncles who were incarcerated and my cousin who was still incarcerated at the time. Should they not experience happiness and love in spite of their mistakes? I realized that some people got caught and others got away for doing equally foolish things. I guess the impression that I made on him was too bad. We were supposed to speak again later that night, but I never heard from him.

I felt rejected. How could a man in prison reject me? What is wrong with me? These men in the South are nothing like the men in Chicago. I tried to act like my feelings weren't hurt, or I wasn't insulted a little bit that even a man in jail did not want to be bothered with me. I asked myself, "Am I acting like I'm better than other people? Am I being *saddidy,* or *bougie?*" As I laid in the hotel bed, I decided to push that out of my mind. Hey, Duke is coming up, and I am going to have a great time. All aboard, next stop is Duke University.

As I got to the campus of Duke, I noticed its historical charm, its beautiful architecture, and well-manicured grounds. Not being a party person, in my mind, I was saying, "Where is the party at?" Although, Duke was an excellent school, I kept wondering if it was the right institution for me. After attending the service in the chapel, sitting in some of the classes and interacting with the different students on campus, it just did not seem like the right fit for me.

As a womanist theologian, I still loved the fact that they had a woman's center and a Black Theology Department. One of my Spelman sisters who went there told me, "Duke wants you, and they will give you a *helluva* lot of money to attend."

I knew it would look good on my resume, and I knew if I started the program, I would go through hell and high water to complete it because I do not quit anything I start, other than diets. I began to have anxiety because it was almost as if there was a tug of war going on in my spirit. I told myself not to become frustrated about trying to find the right graduate school. I will apply two or three and allow God to be God.

When I got back from Duke, I told myself I have a lot of thinking to do. I need to focus on my senior thesis project, and I need to get some clarity about what is going on in my life. Eve went back to Chicago, but she promised me she would not miss my graduation. It had been a couple weeks since the college tour at Duke and I was pushing myself with my senior thesis, by working hard to balance my academic and my ministry obligations while singing on the Atlanta University College praise team.

Eve was my first girlfriend to arrive from Chicago. Smitty and Nisey were flying in together. I was so excited to have my closest girlfriends to share my moment with me. They had been my rock for so many years, throughout my journey of higher education. Eve loved to visit Atlanta, so she came early. By the time she got there, Eric and I had started talking again. It was as if we got swept up in the fairy tale romance between a felon and the college girl. You would have thought I would have made better decisions after the whole "Winston Situation," right. Well, yes and no. I guarded myself more because of what I went through with Win, but I really had not given up on meeting someone special or falling in love.

It was just so different, but we just were attracted to each other and loved talking. Every day we looked forward to talking and finding out new things about each other. It never really seemed like he was incarcerated because he had a cell phone. How many people do you know in prison with a cell phone? There are people walking around in the free world who do not even have a cell phone. We spent every moment we could, talking to each other. He never gave me those jailhouse drawings, carvings on wood, he was not asking me for money, and I was not receiving any collect calls.

I always had a clever story to explain his whereabouts to other people. When I finally told them where he was, some people understood; others felt I was too good to be dating someone in the penal system. As a college-educated Black woman with her whole life ahead of her. They felt I should strive for better. My best friend did not understand it. He said, "Tanell, how are you dating somebody in jail? You can't get to know someone in jail. Dating means, you are spending time with them and getting to know them. You only know what he tells you. You have never spent any personal, or quality time with him." I hated it when he was right.

Eric admired me. He loved the fact that I was educated and in College and he loved to have intellectual conversations with me. Eric always wanted to know about my goals and my schooling. I opened up to him and shared things with him that I never shared with anyone. Eve called me "the track star dater," with everyone but Eric. For some reason when I tried to push Eric away, he would never go. He often told me, "Tanell you are not going to get rid of me that easy. You are the type of woman a man is going to have to marry to keep. I trust you."

I know it sounds crazy, but I did dream of having a life with Eric and that was all it was. I always told him, "You are my moon, and I am your stars." I always saw us having a son together. I never really thought much about having kids. I knew one day I would have them with my husband and that would be that, yet Eric made me want to think about them sooner than later.

At times, it seemed like the very thing that attracted Eric to me was the very thing that irritated him about me. Sometimes, we would get in an argument because he felt as though I thought, or I was acting like, I was the smartest person in the room. I never thought I was the smartest person in the room. He was just insecure. We had an off-and-on relationship for about 9 years, mostly off after two years of dating. Out of those nine years, I only went to visit him one time in prison.

He was four inches shorter than I was and a handsome-and-a-manly-man. He had two teardrops by his right eye. When we spoke on the phone, he told me he had a sleeve. When I saw the shirtless pictures of him, I was like, "You don't have a sleeve. Boy! You have a whole jacket! I cannot take you anywhere. You can't cover those tattoos up with a Band-Aid." I am not going to lie; my first visit seeing him, I just wanted to kiss him so bad and touch him. The next day, when I went to visit him, I made sure I gave him that kiss and a great big hug. He said, "You must have been thinking about that, Baby." I was so new to visiting a man in prison; I did not know that once they came out, you could not touch the inmates after you greeted them. I also did not know you could not take multiple pictures. There were just a few things I didn't know that he had to explain to me.

We had a good visit, although at times I felt myself shutting down around him. He would try to pry, to get me to talking and he constantly reminded me that I was not getting rid of him.

I asked him about the red paint in his tattoo on his hand. I loved it. He said, "That's not paint, Tanell. It's ink." I felt so ignorant. He could tell I was sensitive about me saying the wrong thing so he happily changed the subject. He kissed me goodbye and gave me the biggest hug.

He acted as if he did not want to let me go. As I walked through the glass doors, down the sidewalk, and passed the barbed wire fences, I heard Holy Spirit say to me, "You will never come back to this place." I liked him, do not get me wrong, but it was hard for me to see myself having a future with him. When I met him, he had already been in jail over ten years and he is still in jail nine years later. I saw all the potential that he had, and I really, really, really wanted to wait on him and share my life with him, yet I had to be honest with myself. I could not marry his potential; I would be marrying the man he was.

 By then I knew that God had a calling on my life and that I was going to be a minister. I knew I could never marry him with his background and the type of ministry I was going into. I knew that God could change him, save him, and redeem him if he truly wanted it. Let me be honest, he had been in the penal system so long that he had become institutionalized, doing whatever it took to survive in a hideous place.

Prison really is a modern-day slave system. I wanted to believe that he was changing, but, in my gut, I knew that he was one way around me and another way while he was there. That is what people do; they adapt to survive. I did not want to take the chance on him being one way while incarcerated on the phone and the complete opposite upon release from the system. For me, the stakes were too high to gamble.

For years, he lied to me, stringing me along that he was going to get parole and he was denied every year. One year, I called the prison to see when he was going to be released, and the lady who answered the phone told me, "You are the second woman that has called up here today to ask that question." I never cheated on Eric. When we broke up, I saw other people. It was something about him, at every major pivotal point in my life he would call. For example, when I got ordained, when I graduated from graduate school, when I moved overseas, when I move back to America, or when I had a major job promotion, he called.

In his mind, we never broke up and it was always okay to pick up where we left off. I finally got tired of it and ended it. I ended it for two reasons. I did not like feeling manipulated at times by him, or made to feel like my way of thinking was wrong. I also felt that as long as I held onto this dead-end relationship, I would never be able to receive fully what God was trying to put in my hand.

Pearls of Wisdom

1. Remember, "You cannot marry potential."
2. Never allow anyone to string you along and play on your emotions.
3. Never date or stay in a relationship out of sympathy.
4. There is compromising, which is the process of giving, slightly altering, and receiving from both parties, then there is settling. Love yourself enough never to settle.
5. Never dumb yourself down for others to feel better about themselves.
6. Sometimes you have to let go of what is in your hand in order for God to put what He has for you in your hand.
7. Remember, you can form soul ties with people without being intimate with them.
8. Know that everyone deserves a chance to experience God's redemptive love regardless of whom, or what he or she has done.

Chapter 11

Shacking and Shaking Sheets

"True love does not marry someone they can live with; they marry someone they can't live without." -Aleatha Romig

I had ended my relationship with Eric. I was working hard in graduate school. It was time for me to enjoy myself with the semester ending before my J term began. The weather in the "ATL" was getting hot and sticky as the season was transitioning from spring to summer.

I got back on the chat line with the hope of meeting someone to date and have a good time. My best friend Eve recently had come to visit for a week. I so enjoyed her. She loved coming to visit me and working on her book. She is such an amazing and gifted author. We sat around and had dinner parties, girl talk, and laughed most of the week away. As she was getting ready to leave, I could feel loneliness creeping in and clouding my better judgment.

I had recently started talking to this guy named Angel. He was decent, from what I could tell. We had only been talking a few days when we decided to meet each other at Hartsfield-Jackson Airport in Atlanta. We had seen pictures of each other. Yet, I was slightly nervous because there is always the fear that even though he saw my beautiful pictures, he may not like the way I look in person, or we may not have any chemistry.

Angel had smooth dark chocolate skin, dark brown eyes, and a short wavy afro. When we met at the airport, I thought he really did not like me. He acted more like a platonic friend than someone who had romantic interest in me. We took the train to the Chamblee Tucker train station, and then took the Chamblee Tucker bus to my apartment. We talked and laughed on our way there. I told him he acted as though he really did not like me. He smiled and slightly bit his bottom lip. He said, "Oh I definitely like you. I am just trying to pace myself. I think you are cute, especially your nose and lips. Your nose is really cute." I was not shocked that he said that, I heard that in at least four of my relationships. "Tanell what is your best feature?" To men, it is apparently my nose." I am attracted to you; I will tell you how much later." I playfully rolled my eyes at him.

 We connected well after that conversation. We spent the weekend hanging out, relaxing, and laughing. We ordered in food for the evening, which I paid for because I wanted to assert my independence. Looking back over my experience with Angel, I had a hard time showing vulnerability. I wanted his image of me to be one of an independent, well-educated, wholesome, intelligent, and beautiful woman.

The one thing that he loved about me was my confidence. We took our time before being intimate. We actually enjoyed each other's companionship. He loved to cook. He was a very clean and neat person. The first night we spent together was so chilled, I told myself to keep my legs closed and my heart guarded but to relax and have a good time. Heeey, but not that good of a time.

We sat on my living room floor across from each other, at my beautiful, wooden, butterscotch-colored, coffee table, to eat our fried wings, fries, and pop (soda).

After dinner, we sat Indian style facing each other in my bed just talking. We learned a lot about each other without rushing to take our clothes off. It felt good, real and natural, but I still had to do my due diligence. I had to see this brother in action. The way he slept so hard, wrapped up in the cover on the floor made me think he was homeless. I silenced those thoughts, telling myself you are nitpicking; you are looking for a reason not to date this guy. Can you really blame me after all the hell and high water I had been through with men? I am not trying to make the next one pay for what the other ones did. However, I cannot keep dating the same types of guys with the same spirits, but with different faces. "The devil is a lie and so is his mother-and-law." I deserved better, and if I did not require better, I would never get better. That comes with knowing my worth and valuing myself better.

Angel had to leave after that weekend, but we both wanted to see each other again, so we made plans for the following weekend. We talked often during the week. When he came back the following weekend, he had practically moved in without us having the official talk and him paying half of the bills. At first, I was just happy to have a companion; then, it started bothering me that we were practically living together without being married. He was supportive and a gentleman. When I came home from school, he would have cooked and cleaned. He constantly worked towards his personal goals.

Yet, I had some issues with him. One of the biggest issues revolved around his ambitious goals that did not include a relationship. It always made me feel like we were just playing house "in the meantime, in the between time." We were doing something but calling it nothing. We never officially put a label on what we were.

When I asked, he would say, he really did not believe in labels, as he held me in his arms and Sade serenaded us into lover's bliss. He also did not believe in kissing, which I did not get because kissing can be more intimate than sex. The more time I spent with him, the more I realized I did not know him. He had a mysterious side to him. I could tell he had a rough life. He had done things he was not proud of to survive.

He would walk to the store in the sun to get groceries and not think twice about it. Yet, I lost respect for him when he did not defend my honor when I felt that a white pastor disrespected me. It is hard for woman to be with a man she does not respect. Trust and respect are must have in any relationship.

I had formed a very special friendship with one of my peers in seminary name LC. You would have thought that we probably would be archenemies because of my mouth and my attitude. I distinctly remember making her cry in our spiritual formation class.

She introduced herself and told the class about her family. I felt she could not be effective as a minister because she always lived a cookie-cutter life. She would never reach someone like me who knew what it was like to struggle, to have my lights cut off, to have a family member in jail, to be homeless and helpless. Her white privilege would not allow her to understand the injustices that I and other people of color experienced daily.

She stood up to me in her own way on the verge of tears and said, "You are right. I don't know because I've had what some would say compared to many as an easy life, but I still feel called by God to help those who have had a difficult life." Listening to LC gave me hope that everybody did not struggle as I did, had family members in jail, or had to deal with being kicked out of their homes, or having their lights cut off. It was possible to live a healthy, prosperous and blessed life. It did not mean that you would not have challenges or other struggles. Everyone has them, but it is how you choose to deal with them. Ever since then LC and I have been close friends.

We often helped each other with different projects that we were working on. She was the children's minister at her church. She had done a fabulous job remodeling the children's ministry and that whole wing at the Church. She asked me if I wanted to help with Vacation Bible School (VBS), so I did what any good friend would do, and that was to sign up to volunteer. Angel and I were seeing each other, so I gladly asked if he could come along. She replied, 'The more the merrier, he sure can come and help."

I agreed to take on one of the more challenging groups of kids, having past experience as a youth leader working with at-risk kids. Some of the kids gave them hell and high water because they could, not because they were white people. As a youth leader and educator, I found that children and youth, regardless of the color of their skin, would misbehave if that is what they want to do and if you allow that type of behavior.

However, I set a precedent of mutual respect and honor when I first walk into a classroom. I tell the students I am friendly to an extent, but I am not there to be their buddy. I am there to teach, mentor, and help them be the best version of themselves. I make it clear that I am not their mother, or their sister either. I am there to foster their growth and maturity.

This is why I chose not to refer to people as my spiritual parents, especially as a spiritual father. I have always longed to be close to my biological father; however, I felt rejected quite often and dealt with many disappointments. I cannot even say it was on purpose. I do not think he knew how to be a good father. No one ever showed or taught him how to be. When you find a replacement, or someone to fill that void in your life, if they ever drop you, or leave you, you are going to be devastated if God has not prepared you for that shift and you are not emotionally and spiritually mature.

At Spelman and in seminary, we were taught to use gender inclusive language. Some people may have issues with the maleness of God, and I completely understand it. However, I personally found healing in allowing myself to refer to God as Father. He is a "Good, Good Father, that is who you are, that is who you are, that is who you are, and I am loved by you." There is so much healing, restoration, and confirmation of God's love and God as Abba Father in this song. I have learned that the beautiful thing about God is that God is whatever you need God to be at that moment, not people; yet God works through people.

I am good with working with youth especially at-risk youth. I volunteered to take on the predominantly African-American group of students for many reasons; our children must see more successful, empowering, educated leaders that look like them, love them, and care about them. The last reason is simple; I knew I could handle them without feeling overwhelmed.

I thought Angel and I could do this together as a couple. The students needed to see African-American men doing positive things in the community as well. The students were great! A young lady collected the VBS offering the last day and placed it on the pew in the church hallway. She saw one of the young-African-American-boys in the hallway, who seemed a little startled when she walked up. When she looked at the zip lock bag, she noticed that the five-dollar bill that she had counted in the morning offering was missing.

She alerted my friend, the director of the program. My friend did not want to single out the one kid, so she asked, me "Tanell, can you have all your students empty out their pockets."

I said, "No. I will not have my entire class empty out their pockets unless all of the students have to empty out their pockets. My class is the only African-American class here; I will not make them do that."

As I related the story to my Spelman Sister, another young white female student that we went to graduate school with was like, "What?"

I replied, "Nothing," and I continued talking to my Spelman Sister. "You cannot ask the only group of African-American students to turn their pockets out because some money is missing, and you saw one of them close by. You have to ask all of the students in the program. My sister has two kids, and if she asked them how was VBS, and they said, 'Good, but some money came up missing and they made our entire class turn our pockets out;' the first question my sister is going to ask is 'did they make all the students do it?'"

She had the best intention of not singling him out, but sometimes our best is not good enough. This is why it is imperative to have diversity in every organization, committee, institution, and yes, even the church. Diversity should never be for decoration. It should serve its purpose of creating policies and procedures that are inclusive."

I have never experienced the level of racism and white privilege as I experienced that day. The young lady who asked me "what" misunderstood what I was saying, who I was talking about and what I was talking about. She went to her boss in tears, saying I called her a racist or I was implying that she was a racist. She inserted herself into a conversation that had nothing to do with her. I was shocked and offended as a Black woman and a minister, by the manner and tone her boss, a white male and a minister, spoke to me.

His tone was very hostile and rude. No man in my entire life had ever spoken to me like that. What made it worse was that my partner sat there silently and helplessly as I was verbally and emotionally assaulted through the lens of white privilege. I tried to remain calm under the circumstance and speak to the man in an appropriate tone, but the Wright blood and the womanist in me was getting ready to release the female version of the Hulk.

I politely replied, "She and I both need to talk to you at the same time because there are three sides to every story and we have to work together."

He replied shrewdly, "That's where you are wrong. You don't have to work together, and I am always going to be on her side. She is always right."

He actually meant she was white.

I said, "With all due respect, I disagree with you. No one is always right." By this time, I realized just what I was dealing with. He was a white-racist-fool. No matter what I said, or did not say, I was black which equaled wrong. That was my "Bar-b-que Becky" experience in seminary."

When I went to school that Monday, I could feel and see racial tension and shade thrown my way. I was upset with my partner and my friend. That day I learned that white people stand together, whether right or wrong and regardless of how close they are to people of a different race.

I confronted LC, and she replied, "I didn't know what to say. It was a misunderstanding."

I also confronted Angel, "How could you just sit there and let this white man talk down to me?"

He replied, "I did not want to make it hard for you, amongst your peers."

I lost a lot of respect for him in that moment that I never fully recovered. It was easy for me to forgive LC, but not my partner.

Pearls of Wisdom

1. Never try to judge if God called someone to ministry based on his or her social location.
2. "In all of your getting make sure you get an understanding." Make sure you have a clear understanding on what is actually being said from what you think is being said.
3. Diversity sensitivity training must take place in every organization, institution, and even in the church.
4. Make sure that none of the parties managing the conflict resolution are biased toward either of the parties involved in conflict.

Confessions of My Gender and Calling to Ministry

Chapter 12

Does My Femininity and Gender Offend You?

"If the first woman God ever made was strong enough to turn the world upside down all alone, these women together ought to be able to turn it back and get it right side up again!"- Sojourner Truth

I was in my second year of graduate school at Mercer University. I was finally past the wilderness experience of attending seminary. Most people say, "When you go to seminary, you really go to the cemetery." In some ways, that is true. My professor of Church History depicted this as, "Getting rid of the god-of-momma and them." In doing so, one finds and develops his or her own personal relationship with God for himself or herself.

Many of us have had a wilderness experience; mine was not pretty. I was trying to adjust to many things when I started seminary. I was commuting back and forth to school. I took two trains and two buses to school every day. Some days I did not have bus fare to get there and, on top of that, I felt some of my professors were about two steps away from being atheists. I loved my Old Testament class, but I struggled severely in it. I knew the Bible. Oh yes, I grew up going to Sunday school and learning the Word of God. As a child I went to Sunday school so much I swore when I got older, I was never going back.

Although it was a lot of work, I enjoyed taking Old Testament at Spelman and I did well. My first semester at Spelman and Mercer were difficult at first for me. Graduate school was two notches higher. I had to learn how to approach the Bible from an academic perspective. It was really challenging. I had to ask God to help me and to give me the ability to learn about religions and theology as a scholar. This was difficult for a faith-based person, especially learning how to pick apart the very foundation of faith that transformed my life, then having to put it back together and having to re-learn how to walk by faith. It literally took the help of Holy Spirit, my family, my friends at church, and my community of support to help me through that rough patch in my life.

I had recently learned about a conference that helped foster young preachers called the Academy of Young Preachers. I knew that I had to be a part of that conference. I did whatever it took to raise the funds to go. It was an amazing opportunity. It was in the great state of Kentucky. I went with one of my peers and the admissions director from McAfee. One of my peers, told me, "Tanell, I don't care what you preach about just don't embarrass me."

I went over my manuscript with the admissions director who gave me great insight and advice. I was so nervous I had to call my pastor. He always had a way of calming me down. To be honest, I had never seen him lose his cool. I have only seen him upset maybe twice, but he still maintained his composure. He really has been a great father figure to me. This took time and trust. He prayed for me and calmed my fears.

It must have worked. I received a standing ovation. The African-Americans in the room were affirming and encouraging to me, yet so were the other races and nationalities who attended. The African-Americans understood the call and response style of Black Church.

My admissions director was pleased and he said, "Tanell that was a different sermon than the manuscript I read. It was more of the moving of Holy Spirit."

My peer said, "Tanell you made me proud." I was nervous because I had never preached from a manuscript before, and it was just that, a script. Holy Spirit came in and had His way in that sermon.

Maybe that is the reason why the admissions director said, "That was a different sermon."

I preached on the valley of dry bones and I remember saying, "Oh, but I felt the wind blowing in the valley." I made some amazing connections with many of the other young preachers. Some of those young preachers were offered jobs as pastors based on their sermons.

I had an incident that rubbed me the wrong way. I greeted a group of peers in ministry, not conscious of our gender, just more excited to meet other young preachers to form friendships, foster support, build my network, and, of course, to have fun. I lived to enjoy life. I was among a group of about four males and one masculine-looking female. I introduced myself to the group and stuck out my hand adorned with freshly acrylic nails, the woman shook my hand firm and hard. Her handshake was harder than the handshake of the men in the group. I knew without a shadow of a doubt my femininity and gender made her overlook me, but she respected the men in the circle. Instead of affirming me as another woman, I felt discriminated against by her.

On the other hand, my male counterparts were welcoming and affirming. I discerned that some of her masculinity was to prove herself to her male counterparts. You could tell that she wanted to fit into, "The good old boys club in ministry." In some ways, I had not experienced too many accounts of "intra-gender discrimination" issues that some women faced.

As a womanist theologian, I knew about them, I heard about them, read about them, but I had never personally experienced intra-gender discrimination. I felt like someone was punching me in my stomach. She totally ignored my participation in the conversation. She once "turned a deaf ear" to me by slightly turning her body as she began to talk over me. What she did was not noticeable to my male peers. However, they still talked to me. The group consisted of predominantly white privileged males, but they were friendly, and we were able to engage in a great conversation.

It appeared as though she hated me for grooming myself and wearing make-up as a woman preacher. Maybe she felt that I was giving men ammunition not to take women seriously. This was the first time that I fully recognized the need for more organizations that affirmed women in ministry.

I never really saw a huge need for these types of organizations because I come from a family of women apostles, pastors, prophets, preachers, evangelists, and praise and worship leaders. I resented the fact that she discriminated against me based on my appearance and my gender. I will never apologize for my femininity, my gender, or my calling to be a minister by God. As a woman in ministry, I am very unapologetic for not tolerating this type of tomfoolery. It really takes the focus off the Kingdom of God.

Pearls of Wisdom

1. Never apologize for being who God created you to be.
2. Never alter who you are to assimilate into what others deem as the norm, to be accepted.
3. Make sure that you are not perpetuating the same vicious intra or interlocking system that you have experienced.
4. Collaborate with organizations that affirm women in ministry.
5. Take time to mentor other younger women in ministry.

Chapter 13

"My Gender Does Not Disqualify Me"

"If they don't give you a seat at the table, bring a folding chair."-Shirley Chisholm

I remember at the age of twenty-three getting into a heated disagreement with my Uncle Cedrick because he said, "A woman can be a pastor, but she cannot be a bishop."

My uncle's statement was shocking because he was married to my aunt, who was amazing and a powerhouse. She was the co-pastor of our church, a prophet, and she flowed in the apostolic anointing. He loved and affirmed my aunt as a woman in ministry.

Most people enjoyed her preaching style over his, yet my aunt never allowed that to cause a spirit of division among them. He often pulled on her anointing to set the atmosphere for him to preach. Her gifting and her anointing were so unique. They were not like anything I had ever seen. This is how I learned about the prophetic deliverance, laying on of hands, and casting out demons.

I remember strongly disagreeing with my uncle.

I turned to my aunt and asked her, "Auntie can't God call a woman to be a bishop?"

My aunt said, "I'll be honest with you, niece, I believe God can use a woman, just like he uses a man."

If I had not witnessed it for myself, I would not have believed that my own uncle would have said something that crazy. However, I do not blame him. I blame the organizations and the denominations that foster that form of thinking in which he served under for so many years.

The only way we can get past gender issues or the stained-glass-windows in the Church is by taking time to have healthy dialogue around issues that breed ignorance, and deny others the opportunity to answer the call of God and deny them of their respectable positions.

As women, we have to stop asking for permission to answer our call to ministry regardless of the church, office, or location. Oh yes, in some denominations, women are not allowed to be pastors, or bishops. In the small town where I grew up in, to this day, there is a prominent church in Dade City, FL, where, if you are a woman or a female pastor, you cannot go to the pulpit. You may sit on that first bench in the front of the church, and you might speak on Women's Day at the front of the church. No one will ask you to preach in the pulpit, or to sit with the "good old boys," in the pulpit.

I do not visit or attend churches where I am not fully welcomed or accepted as a female preacher, out of respect for myself, and the leader of that house. If you visit someone's home, you have to keep in mind you are a guest, and you must respect and abide by the rules of their home. Since I strongly disagree with their way of thinking, I would rather not go.

Pearls of Wisdom

1. God does not a have respective person for ministry.
2. Never force your way into anyone's pulpit.
3. Life does not come with call waiting, so make sure you answer the call.
4. Gender basis will always exist, if we have to become intentional in having healthy conversations and taking actions that shatter the stained glass windows in the Church.
5. Make sure you are reflective of the change you want see.
6. Remember someone is watching you, to show him or her how to execute greatness.
7. Remember the contributions that women and girls make daily to the world and the Church. James Brown said, "This is a man's world, but it would be nothing without a woman, or a girl."

Chapter 14

Hero Syndrome

"...No, just be careful of 'hero Syndrome.' Liking someone just because they're nice to you after getting out of a bad situation."- Anonymous

I remember going to see the movie *Why Did I Get Married*, by Tyler Perry, and being blown away. First, my fat pretty butt would not have gotten off that plane. Yet, I remember sitting in the movie theater relating to Jill Scott's character on so many things, especially the scene where she is sitting at the table and talking to "Troy," and she is trying to convince herself and him that she does not want to get caught up in having, "hero syndrome."

She goes on to share what hero syndrome is. She says, "hero syndrome is when a woman confuses when someone is just being nice to her while, in her head, she thinks they like her in a romantic way." Now, it was refreshing to see how he told her that he could like her the same way that she was thinking he was liking her. Too bad, that is not always the case. I can honestly say that was never the case for me.

I cannot tell you how many times I have been caught up in the hero syndrome. I would start liking someone because he was a nice person who showed kindness towards me. The first time, was with one of my good friends. He was a nice person, but he did not have any romantic interest in me at all. Yet, in my mind, I thought he liked me, too. Even other people who knew us from school thought we were dating. I remember when he told people he was getting married; some of them thought he was marrying me, when, in fact, we were just friends.

I think it is easy for people to develop feelings towards others who show them the affection and the attention that they desire or maybe even crave what they did not get from the people that they have romantic interest in or are in a relationship with. Sometimes, if a man or woman take the time to show the opposite sex that he or she is genuinely interested in that person, it could lead to hero syndrome, if a clear platonic line is not drawn.

I remember one time my Aunt Meka came to town, and she met my friend. Anyone could see he was a very nice person and he had a hard time telling people "no." I used to ask him to do all kinds of favors for me because I liked him, and I wanted him to feel like he was needed and important to me. He was just being himself, but my liking him at times blurred my respect for his personal boundaries as a friend. He never told me about what I was doing because his momma taught him to respect women, and he had a good heart. I could talk him into almost anything. John was intelligent, funny, tall, and handsome, with hazel eyes. His worship style was intense, and it drove me bananas.

The first time Auntie Meka met him, I remember her watching me very closely as I interacted with him. She seemed to have been studying my body language to see if this guy was worth all the hype I talked about. When he left, my aunt, who is a shoot-from-the-hip type of person in my Wendy Williams voice "POW-POW," said some very encouraging words to me. She said, "I want you to know that if you are going to be hurt over something, be hurt over something that someone did to you and not what you did to yourself. You like him in a romantic way, but that is not how he sees you. He sees you strictly as a friend." In other words, girl he is not checking for you like that.

I do not really know what it was about him that I liked so much, but I did. I do not know if it was his intellect, or how he treated me. He went out of his way to do nice things for me. I just thought that was a grand gesture of his affection towards me, and it was building towards something lovely. My friend Kami encouraged me, so I was thinking that maybe it could be something there. I drove every one of my friends' crazy talking about him nonstop. All that rolled off my lips was, 'John this and John that,' every time I talked to one of my friends.

They desperately tried hard to see what it was about him that I liked, but they never found it. John was attractive; however, I think I may have oversold him slightly. My friends did not see it in the looks department, and they surely did not see it in his personality; yet, John was unique to me. I think I was attracted to him because of his intellect. I had a documented learning disability, and I had never seen anyone as brilliant as him, other than my Auntie Meka. John and I remained good friends for a while. It hurt me when he began to separate himself from me. I could not understand why.

Regardless of me liking him, we had a genuine friendship that I really respected and liked. At least I thought I did, but the truth of the matter is when I started taking advantage of his kindness, I was not respecting him or our friendship. I felt as though he separated himself from me to prepare himself to be a husband one day. Maybe our friendship was getting in the way, maybe it was dead weight, or was something that kept him from focusing on who he needed to be to a certain extent, but I never felt that way. I knew it was possible for us to continue our friendship while he prepared himself to be a husband. I respect the institution of marriage and would not have ever crossed the line, or made his soon-to-be wife feel anything less than who she was in his life.

I was hurt by the way he severed our friendship. One of my spiritual brothers, Ty, took time to talk to me and to pray with me about how I felt about John. We talked for about three hours on the phone. I remember Ty saying, "Tanell, I don't think you like him, you like the idea of liking him." When he said that, it was as if something in me broke. After he talked to me and prayed for me that night, I no longer had romantic feelings for John again. That was a long phone call, and some might say it does not take all of that, but I am forever grateful for my spiritual brother taking time to minister to me and walk me through deliverance, from being infatuated with John.

By the time he got engaged and married, I was genuinely happy for him. His wife is an amazing woman, whom I love dearly. God did an awesome job putting the two of them together. I could not imagine him being with anyone else other than her. It is funny because now, I am closer friends with her than I am with him. God strategically used her to pray for me, motivate me, and encourage me when I felt like giving up. She and the rest of my close girlfriends became my PUSHERS. To this day, she is a part of a personal group of intercessors assigned to pray for my businesses, my ministry, and me. Had I allowed my emotions to lord over me, I would have missed my divine sister and friend all in the name of having "hero syndrome."

The second time I allowed myself to be carried away with "hero syndrome" was with my first male best friend. I just have something for nerds. I liked guys who were deemed as the underdogs. I saw their unique qualities that others overlooked. I noticed them because for years I knew what it was like to be the underdog or the girl who was best friends with the girl, who happened to be dating the guy that I liked first, that never gave me the time of day.

While attending Spelman, I learned that there were some traditions within the AUC that are a part of its fascinating culture and history. Although Spelman is an all-girls school and Morehouse is an all-guys school, there were times where the mixing of both schools was a few people's main agenda for coming to Spelman. It was to create *SpelHouse* power couples or little *SpelHouses* running around. I remember being so irritated at one young woman the first week of orientation because every time we introduced ourselves and stated what we hoped to accomplish, she would say, "I came to get married."

Dr. T. had formally given us the "this is not the hook up" speech. I was not sure what she meant by that at first, until she began to explain what was about to happen. All the girls at Spelman stood in line two by two and the men of Morehouse met us at the front of Spelman's gates. We were than paired up with a Morehouse Brother. By the time we got to the end of the line, there were not many males left so some brothers received multiple sisters. My Morehouse Brother received three sisters to help support, encourage, party, and to be friend. For his birthday, I treated him to food at Spelman's cafeteria. He came when I moved to help do the heavy lifting, but we never liked each other, or crossed the line with each other. The whole point of pairing us was to build a support system with a brother or sister figure, but some became more than a Spelman Sister or Morehouse Brother.

Being a Religious Studies major, I spent a lot of time in the Camille Cosby Building in the religious studies department. I met this individual named J. J. who stuttered. I found myself drawn to him because my younger brother Jeremy had a stuttering problem. I often gravitated to people who reminded me of him, looking and searching for glimpses of Jeremy. Another fun fact is that J. J. was easy on the eyes, but he had a zeal and passion for Christ that made you stop or stand still to listen to what he had to say. By the time he finished talking, he had recruited a new member of his praise and worship team. Although I am not a singer, I enjoy worshipping God. I also was looking for an opportunity to connect with the community of young Christians in the AUC.

I remember being a little nervous that night at the first rehearsal. Everyone was so friendly and took me under their wing, but I still was a little hesitant about getting to know others because I was the new kid on the block. My first time singing with them was at Morehouse in the chapel. We had to wear black and white. I wore a black and white pinstripe skirt that came to my mid-calf, black stockings, black heels, and a black wrap-around shirt.

I stood next to Chloe who was beautiful in her own way, but not overly beautiful. She was what you would call a plain Jane who suddenly discovered her sexuality and her beauty while she was away at college. She was a church girl who had slightly gone bad. I am sure she found a new form of confidence while away at school.

She was polite, but not too friendly and that was okay with me. I was not going to lose any sleep about us not being friends. I longed for a sense of community and belonging, but not to the extent of sucking up or begging people to hang out with me.

There was a packed auditorium with so many "Men of Morehouse," staff, and faculty members. I was slightly nervous. I was not used to singing in front of people. Singing in the shower is different from singing in front of people. Everybody can sing in the shower but singing in front of hundreds and thousands of people is completely different.

After we finished singing, this guy came up to me and introduced himself. He had the most beautiful smile I had ever seen. His skin was the color of almonds, his eyes were a warm shade of brown, but if you looked at them, they had a hint of sadness tugging at the corners of them. He was clean cut, friendly and welcoming, but the more I got to know this stranger, I would soon learn he was very private and not easily trusting of others.

He said, "You have a nice voice."

I quickly replied, "No, I don't."

Trust me, I was not fishing for compliments either. I love to sing and worship God; I am not a singer.

He said, "Yes, you do."

I replied, "That was not me. That was the girl next to me."

He said, "No, that was you. I heard you. The mic was in the ground by your foot."

Although, I could not argue with him anymore, I was almost certain that the praise team's ability to harmonize deceived him.

It was something about this guy that was different from any guy I had ever met. Each time I found myself in his company, he always came up to speak to me. He invited me to join a praise team that he sang with. The next time I saw him, he seemed a little eager to talk to me. As he reached out and shook my hand, I noticed for the first time that his hands were different. It was funny because his hands never seemed odd to me.

After, we finished he asked for my number, and I watched him type in my number. I could tell that he was the type of man who was hard working, slightly stubborn, determined, and resilient. He typed very fast. Ms. Perez was the only person I knew who typed that fast. She could type about 99 words a minute. Not only did David type fast, he had perfect penmanship. I once complimented him on it, and he said, "My grandmother made me practice and did not allow me to make excuses." I had never met anyone with better penmanship than him.

He was always somewhere silently watching, not in a perverted or creepy way, but in a positive and affirming way. We all often joked about him acting like he was someone's father to all the members on the praise and worship team.

I remember one night we came from Cold Stone, his favorite dessert spot and our friend Carlton was doing the most as usual and David took off his belt and whipped him all over Purdue parking lot on Morehouse Campus. That was the funniest thing I had ever seen. Those two kept me laughing late at night. David became my platonic late-night buddy. We watched HGTV together and ate bacon grilled cheese sandwiches together. I took a special liking to him.

At first, he thought I had a hidden motive for befriending him; I did not. I saw someone who was great but did not fully recognize he was extraordinary. Before I liked him, I baked him some cookies, and he smiled. He said thank you, but some of his friends started telling him I liked him, yet my motives for the cookies were pure. I did not like him then. Many of the girls on the worship team had a crush on his friend, and I was trying to figure out why. He was not bad looking, he was nice, but he was no one I would personally fancy. It became sickening to watch those girls go goo-goo-ga-ga over him. I felt like David was the underdog for no reason and the more we hung out, the more I developed feelings for him that were not mutual.

I always went the extra mile to show him I cared about him and loved him. I was not in love with him, but I loved him as a person and my best friend. We told each other everything, including secrets that we both would take to our graves. God assigned me to be one of the people to cover him in his life. I began to mess that up because of my feelings for him. The whole time I liked him, I dated other people.

I had some unhealthy feelings towards him. I would get so irritated when he liked one of my friends and sang their praises. I remember one night, a couple of years later, while in my first semester of graduate school, I told him that I liked him.

He replied, "I like you too, just not in that way. I kind of already knew you liked me."

I responded, "What! You knew all this time?"

He replied, "TANELL, I know when you like someone. What was I supposed to say?"

I tried not to like David, but it seemed like the more I talked about him, the more I liked him. Someone even said we were going to get married. He saw me for who I really was and understood me. Not only was he my best friend, he spoke into my life and always complimented me. Sometimes by me having a learning disability I had trouble executing what I wanted to say academically, but he could follow my thought pattern. David knew the vision God had given me for my business, Mocha in My Coffee, and always gave me great advice for the empowerment conferences we hosted.

As other friends came into our friendship circle, I felt like I was slightly being pushed out. When I confronted them over what I was feeling, they concluded that it was jealousy on my part and that was not true. I did not care about their friendships, I cared that our friendship seemed no longer important, and that I became just "Tanell." I felt like I was being treated very "common."

A mutual friend said, "Child boo, David, she ain't your girlfriend."

That stung because whatever his feelings were or were not, I am sure it was not her place to say anything because he was my friend. I felt like he allowed our friendship to be hijacked.

The final nail in the coffin for me was while I was overseas working, this same friend knew I liked him and was cooking his favorite foods for him. I understood that they were friends too, but, we were friends first, and she knew I liked him regardless if he did not feel the same way. As a friend, I would have never done that. I learned that not everybody is going to be the type of friend to me that I am to them.

I felt like I'll be dammed if I spend one more day liking someone more than they like me. It hurt me badly; I prayed about it and gave it to God. Yes, he is an amazing guy, but I refused to spend one more day hurting myself. I must be honest; he never led me on. He never said he liked me. I liked him based on the wrong reasons. I expected him to see me like the women he was attracted to and some of his other female friends, but that never happened. What hurt the worse was in my heart of hearts I knew he would never see me as anything more than common. I felt the sting of my words when I told him years later he was "the best thing I never had." That was not me throwing shade; it was me speaking truth.

They say the best way to get over one man is to get under another one. In my case, I was not getting under anyone anymore. In the words of Heather Lindsey, "These legs are closed until marriage!" Yet in record time, I went from liking one friend to liking another.

I was in Beijing teaching, and I was leading a small group Bible study for Americans. My bosses, a married couple, asked if I was interested in possibly leading a small group with another American. They were getting ready to have their first child and needed a little time to balance themselves in that new role. My bosses were two of the nicest and humblest people I had ever worked for. After meeting their small group, which consisted of only Chinese Christians, I found myself in awe of the many luxuries and freedoms we have as Christians in America. They set it up for me to meet Logan, and we had a natural chemistry. There were times that my extravert personality was too much for the introvert in him, yet he had great people skills, so he just adjusted.

Logan's desire was to please God always in everything he did. He impressed me with his level of care and concern for God's people. He was intelligent; however, he was humble, never flaunting his intellect. I remembered we had two guests from Taiwan in our Chinese Bible Study, and I felt that the male did not respect me because I was a Black woman teaching Bible study. Little did he know I have a BA in Religious Studies, a M.Div., and was an ordained minister, yet he did not respect me because of my gender and my race. I have seen this so many times, not just in China.

I was not in the mood for his foolishness. He sat there acting super bougie as if he was superior to everyone else because he thought he was the smartest person in the room. He said he went to Stanford. His eyes widened with shock and pride when Logan said he had attended school there. They clicked. After Bible study when I shared with Logan what he did, he did not see how this guy behaved as offensive. He simply explained it away. I felt that Logan could not relate to what I saw and felt because he was blinded by the luxury of being white-privilege. As a Black woman and his friend, it was the first and last time Logan did not have my back in ministry.

Our friendship opened us up to being more culturally diverse, up close and personal, even though it was more for him than me. I was already a very diverse person. We ended up becoming each other's best friend in China through serving side by side while overseas. Logan was a gifted teacher. I told him he should attend seminary. He had a great job for a major software company. Logan was always nice and pleasant, an introvert who enjoyed the great outdoors. I remember telling him on several occasions this black woman does not hike, does not rock climb, and does not enjoy the great outdoors.

There was one thing that drove me up the wall with him; when we ate out it had to be Chinese food. I had a serious attitude, when I had to spend my money on my days off, on ordering terrible Chinese food. First of all, Logan could read and speak some Chinese and I could not. I was very particular about the preparation, presentation, quality, and taste of my food. I was one of the only people I think on our team who never got sick or had food poisoning while I was in China. When I went to restaurants, I always made sure my food was well done by tearing it apart before blessing it.

One time, I was tired and hungry, and really was not in a good mood; he did irritate me. In his defense when we ate with our small group, we always tried to eat what they were accustomed to eating. I had had enough. He asked me what I wanted to eat, I said, "I don't care as long as it is not Chinese food." Yep you guessed it! Everybody picked Chinese food and not only that, the line was long. We waited over an hour and 15 minutes. Oh, I was very upset, and the food was wretched. Logan and some of the members in our small group knew I was upset. I calmed down some when the food finally got there.

What pushed me over the edge that night was some of the snickering I was picking up on in the crowded restaurant. I just wanted to go back to my room. I left after dinner saying I didn't feel well. Logan refused to make eye contact with me because he knew I was pissed and slightly irritated because of my attitude.

By the time, I got home and settled in for the night, he had called to check in on me. I told him I left early because I was not feeling well, even though he knew that was not the only reason why I left. That was my story and I was sticking to it. Later, when I calmed down, I explained to him why I was so irritated and he understood. I had 250 to 280 students in my large group classes. I attended a Chinese mega church. I ate lunch with my students who gave me plenty of Chinese snacks, which are not so bad. I actually liked all of them, especially the black pickled egg, but I drew the line at that damn pickled chicken foot.

"Look Logan, I don't mind immersing myself in Chinese culture. I love living and working in China, but sometimes I need a break from this food. On my days off, I don't want to feel forced to eat Chinese food, especially if I have to pay for it."

The truth is, it was easy for me to like Logan because he was such a great friend. Yet, I did not start liking him because of that; I grew to like him romantically because, the more I got to know him, I learned that he was the epitome of what I desired in a husband. He was supportive and affirming. I cannot think of one thing that he has not supported me in. When I had my first International Women's conference, he invited people, hung up flyers, donated to it, and encouraged me. After the death of my brother, he checked on me several times. Overall, he has been a great friend.

Later in our friendship, as I began to develop feelings for him, I began to act weird. He went from being my friend to being the guy I awkwardly liked. I never really thought I was good enough for him. I told myself that a man like that would never be interested in me, apparently other people that I shared it with felt the same way. Later, I found out that it was not that I was not good enough, but we were not who God had for each other. Lastly, he was not attracted to me in a romantic way. I equated his kindness to be more than what it was, in my mind. He genuinely cared about me. In my heart, I knew this, but because I was wrapped up in the hero syndrome, I could not deal with the reality of the truth.

Eventually, I got over liking Logan because, again, I realized I needed to like someone who felt the same way I felt about him. In other words, just call me Tina Turner "[I] don't need another hero!" Since Logan, I have been done with developing feelings for men who are just nice.

 The next time, I like somebody; I promise you he will have to show me some signs and wonders that he is interested in my fat pretty butt. What I am saying is, even if I trust myself to know the difference, he is still going to have to pursue me. Through liking my friends, I learned that we must be able to be friends, believe in, and support each other's purpose, dreams, and goals.

Pearls of Wisdom

1. Do not create whole relationships with people in your mind that they know nothing about.
2. Do not allow yourself to develop crushes on people just because they are nice to you.
3. Take time to guard your heart and emotions through the word of God.
4. If you find yourself developing crushes easily, ask God to cover you in that area, so you are not emotionally vulnerable.
5. Write positive affirmations and say them daily to avoid developing hero syndrome.
6. Put some boundaries in place that would not allow you to ruin perfectly good platonic relationships by allowing your emotions to lord over you.

Confessions of Knowing, Learning, Doing, and Expecting Better

Chapter 15

No More *"Randoms"*

"Some of us ask God to show us a "sign" about a guy that we know we shouldn't be with in the first place. God shows you his heart & his rebellion towards Him--and it's still not enough." -Heather Lindsey

I am so over the whole dating scene; I am ready for "my greater" or my "happily ever after." I seem to meet some of the craziest people in the world. I must be slightly deranged myself. "Jesus, com'mon in the room!" I promise you, I am so done.

'*Randoms*' are the people you date just to be doing something. You know it is never going to go anywhere, but you date them for various reasons to occupy space and time in your life. Heather Lindsey coined the term, but way before she did we all have dated at least one *"random"* person. They may be great people, but they are simply not the one for you. The craziest thing about this is you know they are not the one for you, but you still choose to date them and put yourself in danger, spiritually and emotionally.

The hardest lesson I think I've had to learn about liking people is not to just like people, just to be liking them or to hear a deep voice on the other end of the phone. When liking people, you have to know your worth. It is impossible for you to ask someone to come in to love and to fully accept you when you don't fully love and accept yourself for who you are. You deserve more than just a random. You deserve to like someone who likes you equally or even more.

People have told me all my life that I would have to kiss many frogs to get to my prince charming. The first time I heard this, I thought it was ludicrous. I said it out loudly to them, "I'm not kissing any damn frogs to get to a prince." That is what I said out of my mouth and that is what I thought in my mind and in my heart, but my actions displayed something else. I settled for *"randoms"* because of my desperation for love, affection and companionship.

Okay, maybe you do not understand the language of *"randoms."* Please stop settling and lowering your standards by dating people you know you are not supposed to be dating. You know it is not going to go anywhere, yet you do it just to be doing something. That is one of the greatest tricks that the devil uses to distract single Christians because we all want that "happily ever after." We always want things in our own time and not in God's divine time. Waiting is out of the question for us. If you do not understand this, you may understand the story of Jacob and Esau in the Bible. God showed me something that was so profound about the story of Jacob and Esau. Although everybody thought that Jacob was just bogus because he stole his brother's birthright, if you really take the time to read the story and think about it, he did not take his brother's birthright: it was given to him.

It was part of his divine destiny to break a few of the cultural and religious traditions his family had. We know in biblical times, it was the oldest son's birthright to be the first to inherit everything that belonged to his father; except for when God's divine order intervened and trumped tradition and culture. This is exactly what happened with Jacob and Esau. The angel told Rebecca that the younger one would rule over the older one. Remember, when Jacob made a pot of stew, Esau was hungry and thirsty. He had been out in the wilderness hunting, and he wanted something to eat.

We have to tell ourselves it is dangerous when we are out in the wilderness hungry and thirsty because we will do just about anything to be, or get fed. Esau was so hungry and thirsty that he sold his birthright to his brother for a plate of food. Now let us stop and think about it in hindsight. How many of us have spiritually and naturally sold are birthright for a plate of food? When we go out on a date with someone that we are not even interested in just because the person wants to take us out and pay, we are giving up our birthright. (Genesis 26 & 27).

When we sleep with someone outside God's divine covenant of marriage between a man and a woman, we are giving up our birthright. When we take time to date *'randoms,'* we may be forfeiting our birthright. When one enters the institution of marriage lightly, that individual is forfeiting his or her birthright. Yes, Jacob was wrong for some of the things he did. Yes, he was a trickster, but it was part of Jacob's divine destiny to be the receiver of his brother's birthright. The word was spoken over him before he was born as those two struggled in their mother's womb. At birth, Jacob grabbed Esau's foot to say, man what are you doing, you know I am supposed to be first. I beat you at tug-a-war in our mother's womb. Esau sealed the transfer of his birthright to his brother by choice.

Remember that there are eight different types of dream thieves. One of them is the choices we make. To avoid getting caught up in the snare of *'randoms,'* it is important that you are aware of the eight dream thieves; the number one is time. Author of *Dream Thieves* Rick Renner, states, "Time is one thing you can never get back once you have given it to someone you've given them a portion, or piece of you."

Liking men who were not Christians or spiritually compatible with me was one form of randomness I engaged in. They were safe for me because I secretly had a fear of marrying, or falling in love with the wrong person. In my heart and mind, I knew I was wrong for even allowing myself to entertain the idea of liking a non-Christian because I would never give him my heart or marry him. In some ways, I was playing Russian roulette with my heart because I was gambling with the chances of me not falling in love.

Pearls of Wisdom

1. Do not waste your time dating people you have no interest in.
2. Do not sell your birthright for a plate of food.
3. Do not date based, solely on their credentials.
4. Create your list of deal breakers and stick to them.
5. Do not play Russian roulette with your heart.
6. Always make sure that you are equally yoked.
7. Make sure you are not entertaining the number one dream thief.

Chapter 16

The Root of Fetishes

"Many strongholds are a result of an accumulation of uncrucified thoughts and unsanctified attitudes that have ruled our lives during our formative years. As children growing up in a world that is under the influence and the sway of the enemy we received a steady stream of information and experiences that continually shaped us..."-Ken Birks

If one does not guard his or her heart, I think it is possible to fall in love with anything and anyone. I strongly believe that some fetishes can lead to some forms of perversion.   Fetishes do not equal true love. Many times, one can entertain thoughts that, if left unchecked, will stir up desires and feelings that can lead to behaviors that are an abomination to God; derailing us from God's original plan and purpose for our lives. Fetish deals more with a fantasy world of desire, perversion, and lust. It is a world made of illusions where one is always trying to fulfill the images in their mind.

This fantasy world is a severe stronghold that is just as bad as any addiction. I never knew a lot about fetishes. The only fetish I had ever heard about was a foot fetish. While online, on one website, I learned a lot about three fetishes, which were cuckolding, *vorarephilia,* and *macrophilia.* The very definition of a fetish is to have some form of desire towards an object that is not human. There are over 500 different types of fetishes, be careful some can lead to secret sins, and demonic activities.

I have always respected the institution of marriage despite my parents getting divorced when I was a child. I admired my childhood pastor's marriage and knew one day I would be a wife and a mother. As I met people online, I learned about different sexual appetites. One was cuckolding. I had never heard this term before.

I met a man online who was short in stature. He was very successful and not bad looking, but every time I looked at his picture, Holy Spirit told me he was under the influence of a demonic spirit. This guy was into cuckolding. He asked me if I knew what it was. He said, "Did you look it up yet?" The idea and the meaning of it astonished me. Cuckolding allows a woman to have an affair on her husband or intimate partner with his permission. They get to watch, and they receive some form of sexual gratification from being publicly humiliated.

What type of man would allow 'his flesh, his good thing, his favor, his rib, his wo-man, his helpmate' to disrespect God by exploiting her for his sexual gratification? That is not love or sexual intimacy. True sexual intimacy is not one-sided or demonic. It is allowing a couple to be intimate in a way that honors God and each other.

Some people turn to fetishes to compensate for other things; for example, a short man or a man with a disability may want to participate in cuckolding because it gives him a sense of power and control. If they are insecure about who they are or have been cheated on by their partner, this allows them to have a sense of value in the relationship. Some people who turn to fetishes do suffer with rejection and low self-esteem, but not everyone.

I have never really been one to keep secrets from my family and close friends. I knew this was not for me. He constantly asked, "Did you research it yet because that is what I want." I told my Auntie and my sister about it, and my Auntie said, "Nellie-Bell, that aint nothing but some white people into all that craziness. You better get somewhere, sit down, and leave that man alone. He is crazy." All three of us exploded with laughter. Cuckolding was not for me. Even though that guy was willing to give me the world, it was not worth losing my soul, or unraveling that "three cord that is not easily broken." I have never been the type of person who could be bought. Later that week God told me that cuckolding destroys the institution of marriage.

One can have a fetish for an object that is physical or mental. *Vorarephilia* is the type of fetish where one has the desire to be shrunk and swallowed alive to be able to live in someone else's body. *Macrophilia* is a fetish where one is attracted to large people. In their minds, they may be attracted to someone 100 feet tall. *Squashing* is a fetish where a plus size woman lays, sits on, or jiggles on top of a man. This can be very dangerous and even deadly, yet it gives some form of sexual gratification. The first two are mental fetishes. They require one to fantasize or imagine oneself shrinking or being with someone who is abnormally large. The biggest issue with this is in the Bible it tells us to "Casting down imaginations, and every high thing that exalteth itself against the knowledge of God, and bringing into captivity every thought to the obedience of Christ;" (2 Corinthians 10:5). There is a reason why we are taught to cast down every vain imagination because if we do not we allow these fantasies to overtake us. This fantasy world can cause us to lose touch with reality.

Trying to get one's partner to emulate this fantasy world can be very trying and taxing to the relationship. I remember trying to be understanding and accommodating to a couple of guys I met online who were into fetishes and it became so overwhelming trying to pretend to be okay with this role playing and living in this fantasy world. I always thought they were nice, but when I refused to play along in some of their fantasies, they sometimes became rude. Looking at them, you would have never guessed they were into these types of fetishes. Before I knew anything, I was foolishly jumping into this world trying to accommodate and please them in some ways that made me feel so uncomfortable.

It is hard to please people in intimate encounters, who engage in this fantasy world of sexual gratification because it is never quite what they want because of the fantasy they are trying to live out. It takes a lot of work and energy to create the illusion of it. I remember talking to one guy who wanted me to punish him by putting him in a cage, then he wanted me to put him in the cage of my mouth as my hostage. It went from one extreme to another. Now this is not the case for everyone who is into *vorarephilia,* but this was one person I talked to, who also enjoyed inflicting emotional pain. He was like Dr. Hyde and Mr. Jekyll. He had highs and lows of exploding emotional mood swings. He enjoyed the punishment from his outburst.

Eventually, it just became too much to deal with and I ended it. The other guy was nice and sweet, but he always wanted me to engage in this fantasy world of both *vorarephilia* and *macrophilia.* In looking for a normal companionship, I got much more than I wanted. I could not handle it. It was not long before I ended it. I tried to be open-minded and understanding of other people's fetishes, although deep down in my heart I knew that these were demonic strongholds. I tried not to judge them because I knew I was not in right standing with God. Judging them would be the ideal pot trying to call the kettle black scenario.

What shocked me the most about all of this was even though I was not in right standing with God, Holy Spirit never stopped speaking to me or showing me God's grace, God's love, and God's desire for me to be made whole. I was getting tired of trying to be something I was not to experience companionship. It was draining, and left me feeling worthless spiritually and emotionally. I decided that I did not belong to this world because I was a child of the light and it was time for me to come from the darkness.

I knew within myself that instead of indulging in these fantasies and behavior, I should have been praying for those who suffered from these types of strongholds, but my hands were not clean enough to help them. I was too busy helping them engage in their fantasies even if I did not fully want to.

They often did not tell anyone about them. People who are torn between engaging in a fantasy world, secret sins, and yielding to God always seem to be drawn to me. Now, that I have been set free, I feel that it is my responsibility to illustrate God's love and transforming power to them. I have been where they are. Now that we know that fetishes and secret sins exist, what are we going to do about them? The best thing we can do is pray for those who are struggling with these appetites and show them the love of God. I want to be a beacon of hope for them. The rest of the world may see this as perverted or sick, but I see these sexual appetites and strongholds that can be broken through the power of God.

Pearls of Wisdom

1. Always cast down vain imaginations through reading the word of God, fasting, and praying.
2. Do not allow your mind to wander and fantasize about imaginary things and worlds.
3. Make sure you have a stronger accountability partner you can trust, who will pray with you and hold you accountable.
4. These strongholds can only be broken through fasting and praying.
5. Get Christian counseling so you can understand the root of this behavior.
6. Do not allow shame and guilt to stop you from asking for help to get deliverance.
7. Never engage in fetishes to appease your partner, especially if you are uncomfortable with it.
8. Know that most fetishes open a door to demonic activities in your mind.
9. As believers we must never entertain the idea of cuckolding or swinging; they are both a threat to the institution of marriage.

Chapter 17

Looking for Love Online, but Not Really

*"Never chase love, affection or attention. If it is not given freely by another person it isn't worth having."-**Anonymous***

Is there such a thing as online dating? Can you really fall in love with someone you met online? I think if you are open to love, you can. If you meet the right person God has for you, yes, but that is not what some people are doing when they go online. Some people are looking for love in all the wrong places while others are looking for sex with no strings attached. Some are looking for someone to indulge in their wildest fantasies, others are looking for a place to release their inner demons, some are hiding behind screens and keys, and then there are others who are pretending, or will pretend to be anything you want them to be.

Sometimes we can be creatures of old habits, always turning to things where we found comfort in the past when we find ourselves in tense or stressful situations. We end up turning to those old things for comfort because we know the outcome and the solution. Most times, it is a temporary fix for whatever we are dealing with at that moment. For me, that was online dating. It was my go to method of finding companionship. It was simple, quick and easy to do. I did not really have to worry about being committed to it too much if I chose to get out of it.

Online dating is a phenomenon that has swept the world by storm. It became popular in the 90's. Now it is just the thing to do. There is a website for Blacks, Asians, interracial, Christians, elderly, farmers, you name it and you got it. Why? Because people want to be in love, but most of the time we are more in love with the idea of being in love than actually seeking and wanting love. Love requires commitment, sacrifice, and for one to want to give of themselves to someone else. I am talking about the love that's talked about in 1 Corinthians 13.

Yet because we live in an instantaneous society of self-gratification, it seems to be hassle-free to jump online and become whoever and whatever you need to be in the moment. For me, I have been in love with the idea of love for the longest time, but my fear of falling in love with the wrong person has often hindered me from fully sharing my heart with someone. Some of that was because growing up, I had never seen any healthy relationships where true love really prevailed. Therefore, I have always had this image in my mind that there are three types of women: wise women, smart women and silly women. Wise women learn from other women's mistakes. Smart women learn from their own mistakes, and silly women never learn from theirs. I always wanted to be among the wise; in fact, when I pray, I often ask God for wisdom. When I was online looking for love, I could never really find it in one particular person.

I was often skeptical of people because I knew that they were portraying their best representative, so I would do little things to pick apart things they said and did. To see if 80% of their representative reflected who they really were. Some confessed that they loved me, but I needed to see how you responded when the honeymoon feeling wore off. Would they still be madly in love with me? Would they still like me madly enough to stick it out and to grow with me?

After all, I was not trying to be a serial dater. I was more interested in for better or worse. I was never the type of person who felt as though I needed to date someone for a long time to know if he was the kind of man I would want to marry. It only took a few dates for me, and sometimes it took no dates at all, to know if we were compatible.

People accused me of having such high standards for a spouse it makes it impossible for him to exist.

Knowing what I like makes it easier to determine the things I will not settle for. Creating a list has been helpful; yet, it is like a budget. It only works if I use it. Reflecting on the list allowed me to come up with requirements for the future. In order to give my heart and seriously consider courtship, a man must have the following qualifications:

1. Be a Christian, filled with the Holy Spirit, and loves God more than he loves me.
2. Be a worshipper. I found most men who are worshippers to be very in tune with God and the needs of their wives. I agree with Pastor Shawaan Scales, "He must be the five "P's" of our home - prophet, priest, provider, protector and a prayer partner."
3. Never been married and without kids.
4. Be faithful, loyal, honest, hard-working, great communicator, and romantic.
5. Be independent and respectful.
6. Be attractive and well-groomed.
7. Be educated and funny.
8. Be understanding, affirming and supportive of my purpose.
9. Not have a criminal record (**Sex offender**).
10. Must want children.

Unfortunately, this is what I said I wanted, yet I always compromised when loneliness and lust crept in. I never gave guys who I felt did not measure up a true chance. I found something to criticize about all the men I met online while waiting for *Prince Charming*. I will be the first to admit there is nothing wrong with having standards and not settling, but no one is going to be one hundred percent what you want. I think Tyler Perry's movie, *"Why did I Get Married?"* did a great job of illustrating the 80/20 rule. The rule says, "You are only going to get 80% of what you want in a spouse, but many leave the 80 for someone who only has 20% percent of what they want."

I do not think that is a bad percentage to live with if someone has 80% of what you need, want, and desire, in a relationship. If the individual meets the crucial points that one needs and wants in a spouse, then she should accept him if that is who God has for her. On the other hand, if that is not God's plan, then do not compromise.   Too often, we compromise because we think we would never get anyone better. We cannot compromise because we are getting older and think no one will want us, or will marry us.

I have never shared some of the mental and emotional anguish I have endured when trying to figure out if someone was, or was not for me. It was torture because I thought that there was something wrong with me if I did not like someone. I used to make myself like someone by constantly talking about him. Ty hit it on the head: I liked the idea of liking someone, more than I actually liked them. After doing some soul searching, I discovered why I liked seducing men so much in the past.

It was because all my life I dealt with rejection and abandonment. If I could seduce men to get their attention, it made me feel better about myself. I learned that God gave me various gifts to build up His Kingdom; yet, I was using it with the wrong motives, which robbed God of His Glory. I had a natural gift of persuading and drawing people in, which was a form of seduction. This was a gift that should have been used to draw people to Christ; but, was I using it to manipulate and seduce men by playing games with lust and love online.

I had to ask myself, did I really want to be that stumbling block that stopped someone else from reaching his destiny and fulfilling his purpose? I was playing with the duality of answering God's call on my life to be a minister in my everyday life and escaping online looking for love, but not really, and being someone's vixen. This was not what God had called, or established me to be. By denying my divine identity to entertain the spirit of lust, represented a duality of who I was not. In the Bible, it states that "a double-minded man is unstable in all his ways" (James 1:8). I knew that once I came to Christ I was, "a new creature and that the old man [was] dead," but I was not ready to bury [her] and rise with Christ.

For me to walk as a Christian, I had to daily put to death the old man to allow myself to be who I have been fully called and anointed to be, which does not seem easy at times. I had to make a conscious decision to stop looking for love online because what I was really doing was entertaining the spirit of lust.

I met a nice man online who was a hard-working entrepreneur. Our biggest problem was the fact that he was a workaholic. I liked that he was older, a great listener, an entrepreneur, established, a Christian, yet at times I would find some reason to argue with him over little bitty things that didn't even make sense. It was not like an argument of us going back and forth. My lashing out was from my own anger and for no apparent reason, though it seemed to make sense in my mind. I was upset because I told him something he did bothered me, and I felt like he still did it.

One day, after not talking for almost a week, he sent me a nice message and told me, "I think you are wonderful and a nice person, but sometimes you come across as being combative. I like you, and I don't think this is the death of our relationship." I knew what combative meant, but for some reason I had to look it up. When I read the definition, I was extremely hurt that someone thought of me, as "being a quarrelsome and an argumentative person." I learned something new from this individual online. I learned that I needed to work on becoming a better person to prepare myself to be a wonderful helpmate to my husband and that was pivotal.

Sometimes, it is not the method we use to do things, but the spirit or the motives behind what we do. In general, I do not think there is anything wrong with online dating, or looking for love online. However, when we have the wrong motives and are not honest with ourselves, or the people we are attracting, it can be something that can be more of a hindrance than a help to the individuals involved.

My calling as a minister is not something I could take off and put on. Regardless of where I find myself, or what I am doing, I am always a minister. By knowing this, I must always present myself in a manner that will reflect that.

Pearls of Wisdom

1. When dating online you must be careful never to divulge too much about yourself, or give out your personal information too quickly.
2. Remember anybody could be chatting with you from behind the screen and on the phone.
3. Set a precedence of what type of behavior you will or will not accept.
4. Create an accountability system with someone so he, or she knows whom you are seeing and where you are going.
5. If you decide to meet, always meet in a public place.

Confessions of Fault, Hurt, Truth, and Sacrifices

Chapter 18

Be Careful of What's Done in the Dark

"Beware of keeping secrets because surely what is done in the dark will eventually come to the light. It is better to be honest and confess rather that hide from truth."
-D. Smith

In 2010, I had a very frank talk with my pastor in regards to feeling led to be ordained. I never felt like I needed to be ordained to be able to fulfill my calling as a prophet and a minister of the Gospel of Jesus Christ. I did not I needed someone to validate my calling to ministry, in order to walk in my anointing.

However, being in seminary made me want to go through the official process of being ordained, not that I needed it or a title. Putting away my promiscuous behavior, I was no longer living a risky life. I pretty much had stopped getting on the chat line to meet different guys or getting caught up in a lot of online dating. I knew how to live a private life that brought God honor, but I did not know the extent of what I would have to do to become officially ordained as a minister.

I told my pastor, "You don't have to ordain me, but I do feel led to get ordained and I prefer to get ordained before I graduate. I can get ordained in Atlanta or Florida, if you feel like this is something that you cannot or will not do."

He said, "No you are my spiritual daughter. I know your gifts, I know your talents, and I know the call that God has over your life. I have seen your witness, and I have watched the fruit of your labor. I don't want a stranger speaking over you and into your life." He told me to let him pray about it.

I said, "Okay."

It felt like almost a year went by and I had not heard much about the ordination process, so when I asked him again he said, "No, I've been praying about it, and I've been thinking about it. We do an ordination service once a year on New Year's Eve. Do you think you could come for me to ordain you?"

I said, "Absolutely."

For me, this was one of the greatest honors I ever received in my life; recognition as a minister of the Gospel, called by Jesus Christ to preach the Word of God in and out of season. It felt good to ordained before I graduated from graduate school, but there was no real big difference. I have always known that I would never take a job working within the four walls of the church for a salary or based solely on a paycheck.

I knew my ministry would deal more with people outside of the four walls of the church. However, when I was ordained, and my pastor explained the importance of me living a life in the public and private sphere that would be acceptable unto God it really sunk in that I was a minister. He made sure that I knew that I would never be able to go back to living a normal life without the scrutiny of being under a microscope because of the calling and the anointing over my life and my public acknowledgment of my calling to preach the Gospel.

As an ordained minister, one must be careful because he or she does not escape scrutiny of the smallest, most mundane mistake. Most people are able to say whatever they choose to say and whenever with little or no repercussion. I know we are human beings, and sometimes people tend to forget our humanness because we have taken an oath unto God to live a life that is Holy and acceptable and pleasing in His eyesight. Yet people need to remember, in the words of Pastor John Gray, "We are broken and flawed people [too]."

Yes, ministers are generals in the army of the Lord, but when we fall, it is a "black eye to Christianity." For example, it can ruin a ministry for the followers who are under that leadership of that minister. Even in knowing this, every minister has made a few mistakes. After all, we are still human beings, and we all will make some mistakes along our ministerial journeys, but we have to repent and "get back up again." I may have made a mistake, but I am not a mistake. One could say, I didn't know any better with some of the things that I did before I became a minister, but what about the things that I did that I knew I was wrong about, but in that moment, I just couldn't do any better? Sin can be a bewitching and dulling practice. There were times when I wanted to stop masturbating, but I could not, and there were times when I just did not care.

I rationalized and made excuses for my addiction because I was a single minister; I am not fornicating, this is natural, and God, you did not send me a husband yet. Some of us have ignored Holy Spirit, wisdom, and the Bible to chase down the self-gratifying pleasures of our sin of choice. We simply did what we knew not to do for our own satisfaction. It is easy to fall into sin if we do not stay plugged into the source of our strength and deliverance.

Every minister, preacher, pastor, evangelist, prophet, teacher, and apostle has found him or herself in this category at one point in time or another. It may not have been to this extreme, but "the struggle [was] real." They may not ever admit it. Some may want their congregation and the members at the church and their followers to think that they live a life totally sold out to Jesus Christ. This gives the impression that one does everything right.

We know that at times this is so far from the truth. The fact is we hold our heroes and our leaders at a higher level than we hold lay members, so when pastors, leaders and ministers fall from grace or struggle with an addiction, we are so hard on the because they are leaders. We have to remember to show them the same love, grace, and forgiveness that God offers each of us.

As ministers of the Gospel, we have to learn to live an extraordinary life in private as well as in public. This will help ensure we do not have skeletons in our closet, dirt that we are trying to sweep under the rug, or a scandal attached to our names that can ruin our integrity, our accountability, our ministry, and our platform of influence.

We all have done foolish things in our lives that we regretted. We simply must take responsibility for our actions, ask for forgiveness, forgive ourselves, and make peace with the mistakes that we made. Before and after I became a minister, I promised myself that I would talk openly about the foolish choices and decisions that I made in my past that could have ruined my ministry, my integrity, and my accountability as a minister. I would do this not to glorify my shortcomings, but to help others.

The goal is to allow others to learn from my mistakes while I live out my deliverance one day at a time through Holy Spirit and help them not to make the same mistakes I did. I also wanted to be transparent about my secret sins, and the dangers of doing things in the dark.

All of us, regardless of if we become a minister, a public figure, or regular member of society, may have done something that may not be the brightest thing to do in that moment that can cause a rippling effect on our future.

The secret sins and desires we struggle with need to be healed so we can be set free. It is easy for one to say don't do anything in the dark that you will be so ashamed of or humiliated about coming forth in the light. This is, "easier said, than done," but it is possible to do.

Today, whatever date this is that you are reading this passage, make this day, your day of being done with secret sins, and with making fatal flaws that could ruin you, your purpose, your calling, your integrity, your accountability, and your platform. I know you are wondering why ministers would do things in the dark that they know will be crippling to their ministry, if anyone found out. Why would one risk the humiliation and destruction of their ministry? The answer to those questions are simple, as I stated before sin. When one is in a state of sin, he or she does not necessarily care as much about the repercussions or the consequences of the actions because sin has them bound.

It does not matter if you are a minister or a lay member, "The enemy desires to sift you like wheat." If given the chance, he will do that regardless of who you are, your position, your knowledge, or your wisdom. We must constantly sit at the feet of Jesus and allow him to transform us daily by the renewing of our minds. I wish I could stand here and tell you that I have done everything right as a minister, but I haven't, and the truth is I may still do some things wrong from time to time, but I will never stop pressing toward the mark of the high calling of God through Christ Jesus. Some may have sinned or be in a fallen state of being; to those I say, "Get back up again." We all will struggle with something and do some things very wrong. You cannot wallow in it. Repent, get back up, allow God to make you over again, and come out of the darkness as you walk in God's marvelous light.

Nothing good can come from us walking in darkness. Things that are evil and are not of God try to hide in darkness because they do not want to be exposed by the Light of Christ, which brings deliverance, correction, healing, and wholeness. When one walks in darkness, he or she might stumble because there is no light to illuminate the path of righteousness they should follow. As ministers of the gospel, we cannot hide in darkness or play with things of darkness because we are Children of the Light.

We are called to and held to a higher caliber of understanding and living as ambassadors of the Light of the World. Dr. Maya Angelou said, "when people know better, they usually do better."

As a single minister, I liked playing in the dark. I have never been the type of person who went out to nightclubs, smoked, drank alcohol, or lived a publicly reckless life. My vices were always secret sins. My sins were committed in the dark, leaving me unable to grow spiritually at God's pace. As I said before, I struggled with masturbation and lust. However, I never told anyone I occasionally struggled with watching porn. There are many people in church, who struggle with this addiction too.

This chapter was one of the one most difficult chapters to write. There is a thing called being too honest. God, what is the church going to think about me, "the good minister?" Should I even promote this book in church? Am I doing too much? Will people lose respect for me as your delegated authority in the earth? The truth is the average churchgoer does not want to know that the person ministering to them has or is struggling with a secret sin.

Apostle Tammy Willis, asked a powerful question once, "Where do generals go to cry?" I think the generals do not have anywhere to cry because we will not be honest about our struggles, and many ministers do not have a circle of accountability partners outside of their local church that they can be honest with. Many lay members also have this issue within their local churches and communities. They have no place to go where they can be transparent without being judged or condemned. The church is an ideal place to serve as a safe haven for the members who are struggling with secret sins, but what if it is the minister?

I cannot tell you how many people have come up to me, after teaching a singles' workshop, or preaching, to share their stories with me or asked me to pray for them. Some even mentioned that they struggled with masturbation. There are a few issues with masturbation. To me, masturbation means to master manipulating pleasing oneself for sexual gratification. The Bible states that when we commit a sexual sin we sin against our own body and grieve Holy Spirit (1 Corinthians 6:18-19).

I am not saying to give a person permission to wallow in sin because there are some people who want delivered and to be set free. Yet, we the Church, must be willing to show them grace and help them without making them feel like they are a mistake. To let you know as a minister I had these fatal flaws and addictions after God had delivered me, it was hard at first. I had gone two years without dating, I was not suppressing the spirit of lust; I was delivered. Yet, I opened the door back up, and willingly went back to living in bondage, knowing better. It was embarrassing at first until I became immune to living in sin.

The scripture talks about when a man's house is delivered it is clean and swept away and it is empty, but if they do not take that house and fill it, that same spirit will come back with seven more spirits stronger than it. (Luke 11:24-27). That is what happened to me and it is happening to other people too. Some may be world leaders, public figures, lay members, the unchurched, or even ministers.

Some may have been indulging in appetites and behaviors that have almost ruined their platform, the integrity, the anointing and the ministry that God had given them. I am so thankful that it was not too late for me, and I am here to encourage you that it is not too late for you. You serve a God of a first, a second, and a third chance. This does not mean that you take advantage of His grace; it means that you use it to help you live out your deliverance and freedom from any addictions and strongholds that may have held you bound.

It does not matter how long you have struggled with this addiction as a minister or leader; remember the woman who was in the temple bent over for 18 years. She was in this position so long until people probable forgot her name, yet they remembered her problem. The Bible never mentions her name but it does mention she was bent and bound by an infirmity. Jesus spoke the word and she became healed and whole (Luke 13:10-17).

Some of our deliverance from strongholds come through our honesty and having accountability partners to help us live out our deliverance from our struggles of different appetites and desires. It says in the Bible, "We then that are strong ought to bear the infirmities of the weak, and not to please ourselves" (Romans 15:1). It also says, "Howbeit this kind goeth not out but by prayer and fasting" (Mathew 21:17). We, as the church, have lost the drive to discipline our flesh in order to subdue the strongman.

There are pastors and ministers who are dealing with true strongholds, and they are lying about them and covering them up. They do not want to tell anyone because they do not want to be humiliated. Deliverance and healing cannot come if you will not allow God to heal you and set you free from these secret sins. It is the trick and the tactics of the enemy to have you so embarrassed about the sins you struggle with that you are too bound to confess what you need help with by silencing you from speaking (preaching), speaking out, or speaking up to be made whole.

Pearls of Wisdom

1. Find a sacred circle of trust and accountability partners outside of your local church, ministry, business, organization, and family.
2. Daily do a check and balance system with God.
3. Remember to always get back up one more time than you have fallen down.
4. Never use grace as license to sin.
5. Remember as ministers we are not exempt from struggling with secret sins and fatal flaws, so we must sweep, clean, and fill our houses too.
6. Be transparent and honest with what you are struggling with to accountability partners, so they can pray for you and cover you.
7. The Church should always be a safe haven to foster love, healing, and deliverance.

Chapter 19

Loss and Love

"Seeds of faith are always within us; sometimes it takes a crisis to nourish and encourage their growth." – Myles Munroe

The loss of my brothers was something that almost killed me. Each one of my brothers' deaths affected me deeply and differently. It was at two different points in my life. Jeremy's death was pre-seminary and Henry's after seminary. Even with years of Pastoral Care Training, it was hard for me, the minister, to allow others to minister to me, although I knew I needed it. After Jeremy's death, I saw the world differently. I saw that the world could be a cruel place. Jeremy's death was so different from Henry's death.

Jeremy's death was more traumatic because he was murdered, and Henry simply died. No one took his life; he just left us too soon. I was spending time with my play niece. We had planned a niece's and auntie's girls' day and night out. We went to see *John Tucker Must Die*. I will never forget that weekend because that was the weekend my family and my life changed forever. I woke up in the wee hours of the morning and could not sleep.

I could not read my book or go back to sleep. I knew then that something was wrong. I talked to God quietly to myself saying, "God I know when this happens it means that I should be praying for something, or somebody. God, who should I be praying for?" Later, I realized that my brother took his last breath around that time.

When I woke up, that was him telling me goodbye. I got the phone call later that morning from my sister stating, "Nell, they found Jeremy dead on a dirt road. You need to come home."

I felt like the bottom had literally fallen out of my world. I could not breathe. I dropped the phone and screamed, "God, no!" The pain that collided with my reality left me foggy and in disarray. I had to go to church. My body was there, but my mind was in a heavenly realm to keep me from losing it. I felt a heavy hand on my right shoulder. When I looked up, it was my pastor. He laid his hand on my shoulder and prayed me through one of the most difficult times in my life.

We did not know who killed my brother or why. All we knew is that someone had taken him from us prematurely. I knew I had to be strong for my family. My braid stylist at that time was a 17-year-old teenager whose braiding skills superseded her age. She still needed to finish my hair. I had to get her father to summon her from shopping at the mall with her friend so she could finish my micros before our next scheduled appointment.

She said, "You don't act like your brother just died."

I said, "How do you want me to act? Do you want me to cry, fall out, or roll around on the floor?" I said, "That's not me, grief affects everyone differently and people grieve in many ways."

I realized some of her responses were due to her age and the other half of my calm demeanor was due to Holy Spirit keeping me together.

There were moments where I almost slipped off the cliff, but God caught me just in time and wrapped His loving arms around me via a loved one or friend.

My pastor took time to minister to me and provided pastoral care for me. I did not go home to grieve, I went back home to bury my brother and minister to my family. My pastor and I agreed that I could grieve when I got back home to the Windy City. I did not know how or why my brother was murdered, but before I left to bury him, I prayed to God that his murderer would be captured within a month. Detective Leah knew who murdered him within ten days. Two days' shy of a month, she was presenting her case for murder one.

The whole time I was there, God kept showing me a black and white sketch of this guy. When I described it to my family, they said that was the friend my brother left with. He matched the description of the image Holy Spirit kept showing me. Our whole family knew that whoever killed Jeremy was someone he knew and trusted. My brother never would have allowed anyone to walk up on him, if he did not know you and trust you. Jeremy was killed because of what he knew, not for what he had done. My sister still believes to this day that the media caused our brother's death.

I never saw what hurt looked like in a man's eyes until I looked in the eyes of my brother Henry.   My sister stopped eating pancakes. Jeremy always made the best pan-ni-cakes.   She even stopped baking her signature red velvet cakes. I blamed myself to some degree and questioned my anointing and gifting as a prophet. I did not understand how God could show me so much about strangers, but not show me anything about my brother. I was slightly angry with God about losing Jeremy.

One day, I broke down into tears as I shared how I felt with my Grandma Fannie. She said, "Aww-naw Baby. God will keep some things a secret, even from His prophets. Remember the woman in the Bible who had the son who complained that his head was hurting, and by the time the woman got him to the Prophet Elisha, he had died. When he saw the woman from afar, he sent his assistant to ask her was it well and she said yes, but after he inquired around the third time, he could tell it was not well. He said, 'This thing God has hidden from me.'"
(2 Kings 4:18-37).

My grandmother has always had a way of helping me process things and making me feel better. I felt like a weight had been lifted off me.   That night when I was resting, Holy Spirit ministered to me and showed me some of the warning signs that I had received in two dreams. I had forgotten them or did not fully know what some of the things in the dreams meant. I was still learning and developing my gift as a prophet. My grandmother's wisdom helped me have a better understanding and helped me get past the guilt I had been secretly harboring. It helped me stop questioning my gifting as a prophet. I also was able to release the anger I had towards God for allowing my brother to die.

My mother was hurt, but she tried to hold it together for everyone else. We used a lot of Tyler Perry plays to add humor to the delicate situation. My mother suffered from depression for almost four years after the death of my brother. Yet as African-Americans, sometimes we tend not to label it as that or to deny it all together.

She confessed to me she had been suffering from depression for over three years. The minister in me sprang into action and wanted to fix her when that was not my place. I asked skeptically, "What do you have to be depressed about?" She hunched her shoulders at me. As her daughter and a minister, I should have taken time to listen to her, pray for, and point her in the right direction of a trained Christian therapist instead of trying to fix her and judge her.

I was not comfortable with my mother being depressed because I equated her being depressed with her being broken. With her being a former addict, fear used to paralyze me and hold me hostage emotionally because I was in constant fear of her relapsing. I can honestly say with Jeremy's death came new life. My mother has been clean since a little after his death. All he ever wanted was for her to be a good mom and stay clean. I am so proud of the woman my mother has grown to become and the Christian, woman, mother, wife, daughter, auntie, sister, and mentor she strives to be daily.

I have never thought of or knew my mother as a weak or fragile person, so the thought of her being depressed was disheartening to me because I knew the only thing I could do was give her back to God. While in graduate school, I took a pastoral care class and my professor said something profound. She said, "My son Jack's teacher suggested that he might need glasses. When I mentioned it to him, Jack said, 'Oh no mom, I don't need glasses. I tried my friend Nick's glasses on, and that did not work.'"

My Pastoral Care Professor, also stated, "When we look through our own lens to help other people, instead of the prescribed lenses they need, things can get blurry."

For me to look through my lenses to fix my mother was making everything blurry. I had to come to grips with the reality that my mother was an adult; she had to want to stay clean for herself. As much as I wish I could have done it for her, I could not. As her daughter, my place was not to judge her, but to love and accept her unconditionally, just as Jesus loved me.

Jeremy's death was hard to deal with for everyone, especially my mother. I cannot imagine having to bury the child I carried inside my womb, nurtured, loved, and protected. With God, truly all things are possible. Via Holy Spirit, Jesus, family, and friends, God helped us get through that difficult time. Just as we had finally started adjusting and were beginning to heal from the trauma of losing Jeremy, Henry passed away all of a sudden in his sleep. This time I felt death coming, but I just did not know who.

At first, I thought it was my mother or me. I started calling home more, sometimes twice a day. That was a lot since I lived in China at that time. Doop--Doop--Doop--Doop! Ah, snap somebody is calling me on Tango. I answered through my computer and heard my momma's calming yet serious tone in her voice. My mother has always had a way of getting my attention without getting loud. The tone she was speaking to me in was a "listen to me and hold it together" tone of voice.

She said, "Nell, you need to see if those people can send you home. You need to come home. L-I-S-T-E-N." She said it so quickly and sharply, as if to say, I can only bring myself to say this once. She said this in the same tone she used when I was a child and she gave me that one and only warning before she swatted my bottom, pinched my cheek, or "I wrote that check I could not cash!" She said, "Henry died this morning, they think it was a heart attack. They tried to resuscitate him, but he was unresponsive. I need you to stay calm, but you need to get here. I wanted to be the one to tell you. I did not want you to read about it on Facebook." I broke the news to my bosses, and they were simply amazing with arranging for me to leave that day. The company really was concerned about me getting home as soon as possible to be with my family.

They prayed with me and comforted me during my time of loss. My boss Jackie and my Chinese mom came to keep a watchful eye on me and help me pack. I had never seen so much compassion and sympathy from so many different ethnic groups of people. Our team was a diverse, tight-knit family, and as I grieved the loss of my brother, they were right there in the healing process, an ear to listen, a shoulder to lean on, and a partner to pray with me. I think my bosses only concern about me leaving was would I want to eventually come back. They knew I was a great addition to the team and I loved my job, but they still wondered if I would want to finish my contract after this. I told them I needed to take six weeks off to grieve and receive pastoral care, meaning I would have to stay a month or so longer than the rest of my team.

Losing Henry was hard, but I did not feel the same way I felt when I lost Jeremy. It still hurt, but it was a different kind of hurt. Death has a sting to it no matter how it occurs. I kept telling myself, it was just his time to go; yet in my heart of hearts, I suspected foul play. In my mind, I could not fathom how a 34-year-old male could fall dead. I played along with it for my family, but I really wanted to read his autopsy report and see his death certificate for myself, right after my grandmother and mother. I had never seen my sweet grandmother cry, unless she was worshiping God. My sister Nada said that was the second time she had ever seen my grandmother cry. "Grandma balled up her fist and knocked the hell out of Uncle Mike's chest." The reality of my brother's death was almost more than she could bear. They were very close.

My grandma was the only one who could ever talk some sense into my brother. He had her name Fanny tattooed on his left hand and his first daughters name tattooed on the right one. It was something about my grandma's presence to my brother that earned the highest level of respect. He always checked on her and bought her groceries and jewelry. When he turned the corner close by her house, he would turn his music all the way down. Get out the car, pull his pants up, and put his cigar out under the front wheel of the passenger side of his car. Every time she saw him, she started grinning as she said, "Heeey Henry, Henry you *sho* is a good-looking boy!" He would reply, "Hey Ma!" If you ever wanted to see a grown man cry, Henry was the one. My brother would get the water works going whenever our grandma corrected him in a loving and stern way.

Henry and I had a unique relationship. We only had one huge falling out. We both were extroverts and had the most in common. Sometimes, when I was away at Spelman, we would talk on the phone for hours late at night, laughing and cracking jokes. We just really got each other. What really hurt me was at my brother's funeral my sister wrote a beautiful poem about him and their relationship. After my sister said her poem, the preacher said, "Now that one, that one really loved her brother." I felt like he was saying because I recited a poem with perfection gracefully, and I smiled as I greeted people, that I loved my brother less.

I guess in me being me, I may have given him that impression, but I was trying to lighten the mood at times when things seemed extremely awkward. As a spoken word artist, I could not write anything. I tried, so I recited a poem because everyone expected me to do one. I would have preferred to tell a prose story about him or to have sat in the background and quietly mourned the loss of my brother and friend that I had just chatted with online about a month ago. Just before I went to China, he told me he would come visit me overseas, that he loved me and he was proud of me.

I said, "Henry you can't hit the blunt over there. If you get caught with that, you are going straight to Chinese jail and depending on how much you have you can get the death penalty."

He said, "Aww Nell, I am not going to be able to come see you, *cause* I gotta to smoke *evvveryday*."

I looked upside my brother's clean shaved head, looking like thinner, lighter, and a better-looking version of Rick Ross, and replied, "Yep, you better stay here, bro."

I loved the fact that my brothers were always well-groomed men. My brother Henry colored his beard every three to four days. They took pride in their appearances. Both of them always loved to see the women in their lives looking good and treated well. Sometimes when I get dressed up, it is as if I can hear them saying, "You look good, Sis." A playful smile tugs at the corners of my mouth. Every time I hear them in my head.

People often told me, "Your life will never be the same." I found this to be true. When I walked into this McDonalds Jeremy frequented in Carpentersville, the spirit of grief would hit me like a tidal wave of sadness, crashing into me. I would start crying uncontrollably, forcing me to leave empty-handed. After my second time of doing that, my roommate found me slumped over crying in our living room, she prayed for me and rubbed my back.

I told her about my first experience of feeling overwhelmed by the spirit of grief when I walked into that McDonalds. My brother must have gone there or someone who worked there was consumed with grief due to the death of a loved one. The last time this happened to me, my blood pressure shot up. I was hot and sweaty, emotionally, and physically drained. I could not walk. I heard the Holy Spirit tell me that I was throwing my vitals off, and if I did not stop, I was going to have a stroke. I began to calm down. That was the last time that I ever felt that way about Jeremy. I had to make a conscious decision to live. My brother was gone; my dying or having a stroke was not going to bring him back.

I needed to find a way to deal with the fact he was gone and was never coming back. I thought about when he was a kid he would hide in the trees from me. I would go outside looking for him, but I could not find him. I could hear him laughing at me, but I could not see him. I would eventually look up, and he would be in the top of a tree, watching and laughing at me. After a while, he would jump down and scare or surprise me. I always knew he was up to something. Now, both of my brothers are right up there looking down, smiling and laughing at me.

No, my life will never be the same without my brothers, but I refuse to stop living and to wallow in grief. Some people have given up on life after the death of a loved one. The movie "*Courageous,*" did an excellent job with the analogy: "Death is like losing an arm and getting a prosthetic arm. It is not the same, but eventually you get used to it." Although both of my brothers died prematurely, I chose not to allow myself to be consumed by grief rather; I chose to honor them by celebrating their lives and living mine to the fullest. My life will be an adventure every day because both of theirs were cut short.

Pearls of Wisdom

1. "Always remember to give people their flowers while they are living."
2. Remember if you look hard enough, with death comes new life.
3. Take time to grieve and celebrate the life of a loved one.
4. Never try to fix people as ministers based on our own personal prescription.
5. Do not allow the loss of a loved one to consume you to the point where you stop living.
6. Do not slip into a pattern of just existing day by day. That is not what that loved one would have wanted for you. They would want you to live your life to the fullest.
7. Remember everyone grieves differently. Be careful about what you say and do in terms of encouraging, ministering, and caring for individuals during the loss of a loved one.

Chapter 20

It's Lonely at the Top

*"Lots of people want to ride with you in the limo, but what you want is someone who will take the bus with you when the limo breaks down." - **Oprah Winfrey***

I promise you it is not you; it is me. I just know what I am looking for, and I am sorry you are not it. I do not mean to sound arrogant, or narcissistic. I just know that my being with him would alter my destiny and ruin his life. How do you say to a person that they are, or you are, not God's best option for each other?

I have had to make some serious sacrifices for the sake of the call and the anointing over my life. When we are not strong enough or brave enough to cut things and people off, that are not a part of our purpose and destiny, God will allow us to fall out of favor with them, or have them cut us off. Thank you, God, for the pruning process, thank you for removing the weight, and the bulk that separates me from you.

It is lonely at the top. If you think I am telling a lie, ask any minister, leader or effective change agent. There are times when you have to do what you do not necessarily want to do. There have been many times that I have had to give up relationships and friendships that would have altered God's purpose and calling over my life.

I remember, while overseas, I started dating a young man by the name of Si. He loved God, he knew that God had called him to be a minister, and he was actively looking for a wife. However, the wife that he wanted was going to help him be the next Bishop T.D. Jakes, Creflo Dollar, and Kenneth Copeland. I do not know exactly who, but he had these radical ambitions of becoming somebody with a mega-ministry.

I was not aware of Si's intentions because we started out as just friends. He would ask me questions to get my opinion on how to expand his ministry, and how I would do certain things. I was always honest and upfront with him. One day, he confessed to me that he knew most of the answers to the questions he was asking me. He simply wanted to know my opinion and thoughts pertaining to that subject.

He said he was looking for someone with whom he could build a ministry. I was flattered, I mean what is there not to like about Si? He was a Christian, a worshipper, hardworking, funny, and passionate about serving God. He met most of the requirements on my list of potential things I wanted in a spouse. The only thing about Si, I could say I did not like was that physically we did not look very compatible for each other. I was 6 ft'1 and 444 lb. I towered over him in height and dimension. He was a scrawny little African man who loved God, and I told myself that was enough for me. If he loved God and he loved me and met all of the other requirements on the list, I could do without having somebody of my stature.

I am going to have to talk myself into looking down to say, "Honey, how was your day," instead of looking up like I always imagined. I had to tell myself it is okay to settle, if he can lead and truly be the head of our household, I will look down every day. We had great chemistry, we got along, we laughed most of the time and enjoyed each other's company.

One day, I asked him if my size was an issue for him."

He said, "No."

I said, "One of us is going to have to do something about our size. Either I'm going to have to lose some weight or you are going to have to gain some." We both started laughing about the irony of it.

He said, "I am African, it is in my nature to be small and skinny," and on that note, the laughter erupted from us again. I was all set to enjoy something new and creative with Si.

I remember the first time he came to visit me at my dorm. When he came in, I quickly locked the door behind him, not paying any attention to one of my co-workers walking down the hall. Seeing me lock the door behind him, made me a target of her joking. She said, "Tanell, you locked the door pretty quickly. What were you all doing in there?" It could have smeared my image as a minister and a Christian if the people I worked with had not seen me live as Christian on a daily basis.

For the first time, I truly knew what that scripture meant, "Let not then your good be evil spoken of: For the kingdom of God is not meat and drink; but righteousness, and peace, and joy in the Holy Ghost" (Romans 14:16-19).
Although we simply hung out, talked, cuddled, and watched a movie, she would have never believed that that was the only thing we did.

Sometimes, I resented the fact that I was a prophet with a keen
spirit of discernment. Holy Spirit began to whisper in my ear
that he was not the one. Ignoring the Holy Spirit, I tried to
silence the whispers, but then He began to show me glimpses of
the woman Si would marry. I got upset with God, and I began
to debate this in my mind telling God this is not fair. Every time
I seemed to meet someone nice who was a Christian, a
worshipper, and had something going for themselves, God
came along and messed things up talking about, "He's not the
one."

Who is ever going to be the one? You know I am not getting
any younger. The truth of the matter is; I was tired of God
rejecting everybody that I thought was a great suitor for me. Si
was pretty much everything I was looking for, except I was not
physically attracted to him. I told myself I am okay with looking
down at him, as I greet him daily when he comes home from
work, opposed to looking up and asking, "Honey how was your
day?" I knew I was settling, but I did not mind as long as I
could trust him to be "a man after God's own heart." Could he
be tall in the spirit is what I question?

The more I thought about it, the more I desired him to be
someone I could do more with other than just build ministry. It
was essential for him to meet the perfect partner to build
ministry with. For me, I wanted to meet the divine partner God
had designed me to be with before the foundation of the world.
I did not want to get married just for somebody to respect me as
a minister or to be a ministry building partner, but I wanted to
experience true love.

For far too long single ministers have gotten a negative rep and have been pushed and forced into loveless marriages to be promoted, to different positions, titles, and offices within the church. Some single ministers are deemed as burning with lust and unstable, when compared to married ministers. These are stereotypes that could also be said about those who are married.

There are churches, pastors, and leaders that prefer and favor married couples over singles and this does not just apply to single ministers. Yes, marriage is a blessing and, yes, it is a ministry, but so is the gift of singleness. Apostle Paul said, "For I would that all men were even as I myself. But every man hath his proper gift of God, one after this manner, and another after that. I say therefore to the unmarried and widows, it is good for them if they abide even as I" (1 Cor. 7:7-8).

People will ask the most random questions pertaining to singleness or have the most bizarre reason why that person is still single. My great-grandmother is 105 years old and every time she sees me, she asks me the same questions "You still single? You ain't married yet? You ain't got no kids. What you are waiting on? You do want a husband, don't you?" When I reply yes that I'm still single, she always acts so surprised, "You is…. naaaawww!"

"I am waiting for God to send me a husband and that is why I don't have kids. Trust me, I am actively waiting."

"Mmm, that's good."

Now Great Granny-Granny gets a pass. She is a hundred and five years old, but other people need to stop asking single people, especially single ministers, why they are not married yet, or assuming there is something wrong with them. I cannot tell you how many times I have been asked some of the craziest questions. For the love of God, and all that is holy, no I am not gay, no I do not have a problem being married, no there's nothing wrong with me. I am not single because God is working on me, nor am I single because I need to get settled.

I am single because I have not yet met the man God has intended for me. I do not believe that I have to compromise who I am, what I am, or what I like, in order to be married. People have too many preconceived assumptions about marriage. Some people settle because they feel the need to be married. Some feel as long as both are Christians they are not settling. Well, we see how that has been going in the church.

Marriage is much more than that to me. Marriage should not just be about building a ministry, or being reduced to marrying who likes you. For me, I want to marry the person who God created me to be with before the foundation of the world. I need someone who understands my purpose, my passion, my calling and one who will push me to execute the greatness that God has put inside of me. Most of all someone I honored to be selfless for without them demanding it of me.

He has to be my friend that I can love and cherish for the rest of my life and, yes, things won't be peaches and cream every day, but he would be somebody I am willing to fight for on a daily basis. I want to be everything he needs me to be or at least very close to it. Some people allow others to talk them into settling for the sake of a ring. I know many women who went to seminary just to find a husband, and although they got a husband, they did not get what God had in mind for them.

Outside pressure from other people started making me think that something was wrong with me because my biological clock was not ticking. I told myself maybe it was ticking, and I was pressing the snooze button out of fear. I told my mother if I did not marry by forty, I was strongly considering having artificial insemination. I want to experience at least being a biological mother once.

It was prophesied to me when I was getting my hair done for prom that I was going to have a good husband. She saw me with a child, but she did not see more than two. At 38, I do not plan to have more than two. It is funny because no matter what I was doing, or where I was, if someone was talking about God, I was all ears.

One day, I sat quietly eavesdropping on the conversation my stylist and her other client were having over my head.

The client turned to me and said, "I'm sorry."

I said, "No you are fine, I am listening. I always listen when people are talking about God."

She then told me, "Don't be nervous, it is going to be all right." She discerned my anxiety about going to prom and that is when she began to prophesize to me.

My mother never responded when I told her about my plan. She just listened intently, discerning God's divine will for my life. I had thought about this long and hard and I knew my momma was going to want to hear a well-thought-out plan and the why factor, so, I hit her with the BOOM and laid out a well-crafted argument. She looked at me slightly impressed as I gave my closing argument. She has always told me I should have been a lawyer. Heeey, do not get me started. I was planning on being the next Star Jones at one point in time in my life. Even considered it my last year in seminary, but let me just say God had other plans for this single minister.

About a week later, I was sitting and having coffee with my beautiful mother. I shared with her that I decided to wait until I got married to have kids. She said, "emmm" as only she could. I said, "I have waited all these years, for God to send me a husband before I start to have kids. I think to go ahead of God would make my waiting in vain." My mother smiled, agreeing with me whole-heartedly.

She said, "emmm, I agree."

I said, "I am going to have faith, and trust that God will bless me with the right husband, and in God's timing, we will have children."

People always ask me if I want kids and I say, "Yep, but I don't have a husband."

"So what does that mean?" they ask and might even say, "And?"

I tell them I choose to be married before I bring a child into this world. What the next woman chooses to do with her body that is between her and God. You have a lot of excellent single mommas out here who never got married, want to get married, don't want to get married, and I applaud them because regardless of the case they are busting their butts to take care of their babies. You have some who waited to get married and still ended up being a single parent. The worst case for me is when I see married, but single parents. You are the parent and, or the spouse, who is always talking about "my husband this," or "my wife that" but you are struggling or living the life style of a single person. No, you should have just taken the time to embrace your singleness."

Single ministers are more than capable of doing more than just being married and being a minister. I am capable of being single and a minister. Please don't ask me to compromise with my calling for a ring. In doing so, you ask me to, "Say Yes to the Dress" and no to the ministry. Some single ministers are made to feel there is something wrong with them if they choose to say no to the dress and yes to ministry. I am a multi-faceted being. "I Can 'Say Yes to the Dress'" and yes to ministry all in God's divine time.

Pearls of Wisdom

1. Due to the call of greatness over your life, you are going to have to make some sacrifices.
2. Make sure your motives and other's motives are right for dating each other.
3. Do not allow anyone to pressure you into getting married or having a baby, if you are not ready.
4. Do not get married for titles or positions.
5. Do not rush your single season to get married.
6. John Gray states you should marry "purpose over preference and substance over surface."
7. Be careful how you ask people why they are not married and why they do not have children. They may want those things and are having problems with meeting the right spouse, they could be trying to get over a bad break up, or they may be having trouble conceiving.

Chapter 21

Reflecting on My Confessions

"A confession has to be a part of your new life."-**Ludwig Wittgenstein**

I was sitting quietly, reflecting on God's love, grace, and my calling to ministry. Why He chose me is still baffling. All I know is that He uses imperfect people every day to turn this world upside down. As long as I live, I will strive to live a life that brings Him glory and work to be a servant and minister of the gospel.

Writing this book often felt risky and painful, requiring me to be vulnerable and brave simultaneously. This confession had to be (H.O.T.) "honest, open, and transparent," in the words of Pastor Mike Todd. In order for me to embrace my journey of healing and wholeness. I had to confess the shame and guilt, that for years, has held me emotionally hostage and combative.

At times, it was hard for me to admit as a woman and a minister that I struggled with secret sins that have almost destroyed my integrity as a minister, yet God still loved me enough to give me an opportunity to take this transformational journey. Confessing my secret sins has changed me as a person, a woman, and as s minister.

It was when I started confessing to Jesus and allowing the Word and the love of God to wash over me that something began to shift within me. God started teaching me how to truly love myself. God showed me that in order for me to be able to tackle the deep-rooted pain and traumas I suppressed most of my life; I would have to allow forgiveness to be my healing balm.

This memoir has provided a place for me to be transparent about the strongholds I have struggled with and provided me with a platform to encourage others to do the same. Holy Spirit equipped me with courage and boldness needed to tell my story so that I could take dominion over the secret sins that had held me captive. It helped me create a support system of accountability, enable me to flourish, and allowed me to have the freedom to answer my call to ministry.

Reflecting on my confessions has been therapeutic. It has helped me identify and work on my personal and spiritual goals, so that I can help others to become set free from the shame and guilt of their secret sins, that may have left them feeling unworthy of God's love. God is ready to make you whole, are you ready to confess?

Pearls Wisdom

1. Never think that you are too deep in sin for God to love and deliver you from your struggles.

2. Never allow your title or position stop you from confessing and seeking God's help daily to maintain your deliverance. Example: praying, fasting, journaling, worshiping, healthy fellowship with the Church, reading the Word of God, and being intentional in listening and talking to God.

3. Take at least one sabbatical a year.

4. Do not allow secret sins to feaster by trying to hide them or trying to suppress them.

5. Share with your inner circle what you are struggling with and allow them to hold you accountable.

6. Get counseling, pastoral care, and life coaching to help you work on your mental, emotional, and spiritual wellbeing.

7. Make sure that you take time to get ministered to as opposed to always ministering to others.

8. Make sure you set personal and professional boundaries.

Confessions of The End of the Book Discussion

Chapter 1: Blemished Fruit
Why do you think the author shared her blemishes so soon in the book?
How do we hide and mask our blemishes?

Chapter 2: Things My Daddy Did and Did Not Do
Do you think if, the author's Dad would have been home more and active in her life, she would not have gotten abused?

Chapter 3: The Monster in My House
Why do you think the author's mom stayed with Jackson?
Do you think Jackson was fooling Great Granny-Granny?

Chapter 4: I Come from Good Stock
Do you think Fannie was right about God being a God of color and having a sense of humor?

Chapter 5: My Mama Told My Secret
Do you think the author's momma should have told her secret?
Do you think Drake was trying to take advantage of Tanell?

Chapter 6: "I Can Do Bad All by Myself"
Do you think Darnell really wanted to marry the author?
Do think God honored her request?

Chapter 7: My Muse
Do think My Muse mental issues were rubbing off on the author?

Chapter 8: Deliverance has Come
Do you think Tanell was really delivered from lust?
Why did God have to affirm to the author that He called her?

Chapter 9: Saving Grace
Do think you think the author was being naïve about Winston?

Chapter 10: Looking for Mr. Right, but Settling for Mr. Wrong
Do think the author should or should not have given Eric a chance?

Chapter 11: Shacking and Shaking Sheets
Do you think the author was wrong for practically living with a guy while in seminary?

Chapter 12: Does My femininity & Gender Offend You
Do you think women should try to down play femininity when they accept the call to ministry?
Do you think the author should have called the girl out that was rude to her for being a feminine-looking preacher?

Chapter 13: My Gender Does Not Disqualify Me
Do you think that there are still stained glass windows in the Church?
Do you think the author's Uncle Cedrick was telling the truth about women being bishops in the church?

Chapter 14: Hero Syndrome
Have you ever had a case of hero syndrome?
Do think the author was wrong for being upset about her friend cooking for the guy she liked?
Did you think that John, David, or Logan may have made the author think that there was more going on with them than there was?

Chapter 15: No More *Randoms*
Did you agree with the author that dating *"Randoms"* can lead to the number one dream killer?
Why do you think people date *"Randoms?"*
Do think some people have *"Ismael Syndrome?"*

Chapter 16: The Roots of Fetishes
Do you think fetishes are demonic?

What do you think about cuckolding?

Chapter 17: Looking for Love Online but Not Really
Do think single ministers should do online dating?
Why do you think the author really dated online?

Chapter 18: Be careful of What's Done in the Dark
Do think ministers who struggle with secret sins should still be allowed to minister? If so, are there any stipulations?
Do you think the author told too much of her business to ever be taken seriously as a minister?

Chapter 19: Love and Loss
Do you think depression is normal after the death of a loved one?
Do you think the author was too hard on her mom?

Chapter 20: It's Lonely at the Top
Do you think the author should or should not have changed her mind on artificial insemination? Why or why not?
Do you think married people are valued more in churches and in organizations? If so, why or why not?

Chapter 21: Reflecting On My Confessions
Do you think the author was right for confessing?
Are you ready to confess?

Coming Soon!

Made in the USA
Columbia, SC
03 February 2019